POETS OF THE DANIEL PRESS

COLIN FRANKLIN

Poets of the Daniel Press

RAMPANT LIONS PRESS

1988

The Rampant Lions Press

12 Chesterton Road, Cambridge, England

ISBN 0 902591 19 3

Printed and made in Great Britain

FOREWORD

My purpose is to recall a few poets who are seldom read. 'In the summer term of 1890', wrote Laurence Binyon in the *University of Toronto Quarterly*, April 1939, 'when I was half-way through my time at Oxford, I was invited by the President of my College and his wife (Margaret L. Woods, the poet and novelist), to dine and meet Robert Bridges, whose name I then heard for the first time. The President had a cottage on Boar's Hill, the only house then existing on that heathy ridge which has since become thick-sown with the dwellings of dons and poets'.

The conversation turned upon Gerard Manley Hopkins, who had died in Dublin the year before. He and Bridges had been undergraduates together, Bridges at Corpus, Hopkins at Balliol. Binyon called his article *Gerard Hopkins and his Influence.* That evening on Boar's Hill was gathered, in conversation or influence, the soul and spirit of the Daniel Press: Binyon, whose volume of poems would be printed there five years later, invited by the President of Trinity and his wife Margaret Woods who wrote for the Press; meeting at dinner Bridges whose taste and choice presided over such poets as entered the small circle; discussing Hopkins whose works so nearly appeared there, instead of waiting another quarter of a century until Bridges felt the time had come.

'We dined at this cottage', Binyon wrote, 'and walked down after dinner in the midsummer twilight'. Almost unimaginable now, a century on. You drive round the one-way system, through traffic lights and past the Park-and-Ride to the roundabout, along a stretch of by-pass, over the new A34, up at last to the beginning of Bagley Wood from which, if you look back, you may ignore suburbia and lines of pylons with their loops of cables, to view in the mind's eye that focal Oxford, still existing, as those three saw it in midsummer twilight. The walk down might yet be possible, with a glimpse of Ferry Hinksey and up Walton Well Road.

Several temptations lead towards the Daniel Press. I remember choosing my first Daniel book many years ago at Quaritch, *Poems by Henry Patmore*, Coventry Patmore's son who died very young of tuberculosis. The delicate quarto, bound in slate-grey morocco by Morley of Oxford, might stand as one symbol of Daniel's work: minority taste, a minor talent, only likely to reach a few, brought to the printer by Bridges with whom the elder Patmore, Hopkins, and one other Daniel Press poet, Richard Watson Dixon, seemed to be forging new rules for English prosody about which they exchanged long critical technical letters.

My habit grew, as it could in those days because Quaritch must have found by chance more than one largish Daniel collection. Though rare, none of these books could be expensive except *The Garland of Rachel*, and I had to wait for that. This is not to develop into the story of my collection. The many charming books, all slender and most rather awkward because of overlapping printed paper covers, assembled until I sold some after turning bookseller, perhaps regretting their departure. A friend in New York had said 'If you become a bookseller you must be ready to part with your best books', and for better or worse I listened. Though not 'best' in the sense of most precious, Daniel books must always be uncommon, and away they went.

By good luck and the courtesy of Hylton Bayntun-Coward a better collection came back, and to this I have added, until an almost complete collection of the Daniel Press at Oxford is now on my private shelves, from 1874 until the printer decided to finish that happy activity after becoming Provost of Worcester College; lacking certain of the unobtainables but including others, with a few examples from his printing as a boy at home, and the box of minor pieces given by Falconer Madan, bibliographer of the press, to St John Hornby.

As one folly of collecting is fear of disappointment if a book becomes too thoroughly explored – better not handle the dried flesh of a saint, defended by its reliquary – often books wait too long for recognition. Two decades ago I answered an invitation to address the Double Crown Club by proposing as subject 'Robert Bridges, Poet of the Private Presses'; but I had not then read Bridges with care, and Double Crown members expected a typographic theme. I chose *Golden Asses at the Private Presses*, and enjoyed studying Apuleius in translation.

Bridges has stayed in my mind, nagging ever since. Eight volumes of his own poems appeared in small editions at the Daniel Press*, as the small world of such collectors knows, and he brought his friends into that treasured tribute to Daniel's one year old daughter, *The Garland of Rachel*. Thirty-six copies of

*I count the five parts of *Shorter Poems* as one.

The Garland were printed; I had owned it twice but three impossibly tempting volumes came into Christies at one of the Houghton sales, including that which had belonged to Robert Bridges. I bought all three, by the generosity of friends who knew my anxiety; the other two Houghton books, handsomely bound – I could not believe the sight when that group was exhibited at Christies in New York – were proofs and correspondence for *The Garland*, and a manuscript copy of the book, with letters from the poets, the strange creation of a Dundee enthusiast called Falconer, recorded in Thomas Mosher's reprint of the book: 'Mr C. M. Falconer, of Dundee, who despaired of ever meeting with a copy in the way of trade, or of being able to buy it though it did turn up, was so desirous to obtain one to complete a certain section of his library that he hit upon the happy thought of making one for himself...'

Most of the Daniel Press publications, in a minor key, compare visually with Hornby's early Ashendene books. The two printers corresponded; Hornby viewed this as the only private press to run along the same lines as his own. Too much has been written about Fell type*, used by both printers; it will be mentioned as little as possible in this essay. Each of the paper-covered books is safe in its titled folder made by Alan Winstanley. A few others have charming bindings made in their day by Emily Daniel, Katherine Adams, Morley of Oxford. An excuse for keeping them all these years arrived when my son Noah chose Worcester as his college, so it seemed appropriate that one day he should own the Daniel books. Now his son Charles is born; so in the hope that my Daniel Press collection will thereby remain one more generation in the freedom of private care, beyond institutional prison, this short book is dedicated to my grandson Charles Roger Noah, whom as these sentences are written I have not yet seen, trusting he may in his turn own and cherish it.

But one point in writing this essay far from home is that it cannot become the history of a collection. Bridges enters, though it is with scepticism I watch him at first; for there is a temptation in returning to the out of taste, which makes critical response unreliable. Daniel, Oxford, Worcester College, Bridges on Boar's Hill, the almost forgotten names: Dixon, Mary Coleridge,

*The matrices were brought from Holland in late seventeenth century & on the initiative of Dr Fell, Dean of Christ Church, for use at the University Press; they are still there.

Warren, Margaret Woods. Was this wish to discover their world again only a retreat, a withdrawal beneath the leaves as if those pylons and the roundabouts, A34, the Park-and-Ride, were not yet made?

The merits of Bridges as a poet, one would think, are beyond range of debate; but apart from the critics who continue to write books about him, who reads Bridges? 'Today', Brett Young wrote in 1914, 'it feels to me almost an impertinence to quote examples from many poems which have become part of our poetic consciousness'. Three-quarters of a century on, if we have a poetic consciousness, his poems form no part of it. 'London Snow' lives in anthologies, 'On a Dead Child' also perhaps, and there he ends. Almost six decades ago *The Testament of Beauty*, four thousand lines of it appearing on his eighty-fifth birthday, within two months 'ran very quickly into 5 figures', as he put it, 'and is still running'.* Few are likely to spend time or money upon it now.

It may always be possible to re-enter the out-of-taste; perhaps no neglect of art which was once admired is valid, no reason exists for supposing we now know better. That which was once enjoyed is there for our pleasure still.

Most of the poems reprinted here appeared first at the Daniel Press; where that is not so, the point is noted. The form Bridges', Hopkins', Woods' is used, rather than Bridges's, Hopkins's, Woods's. As several friends thought more should be provided to introduce Daniel and his press, I have lazily inserted in the introduction passages from the Daniel chapter of my book *The Private Presses* (pp 13-16 below).

I am most grateful to the Provost, the Department of English, and especially the Special Collections staff at the University of Tulsa, Oklahoma, where this essay was written in a pleasant and peaceful autumn; to the Librarian of Worcester College, for courteous access to Daniel's correspondence; to Sebastian Carter who has not only produced the book in his own idiom but made many helpful editorial changes; and to Charlotte, as ever, who has lived with my small theme and encouraged me to follow it.

COLIN FRANKLIN

*Letter to Edward Thompson of Oriel, *Robert Bridges*, p. 118.

INTRODUCTION

In the history of private presses, contemporary literature has not taken first place. William Morris printed his own poems (most had appeared before) and a volume by Wilfrid Blunt; no new verse was printed at the Doves Press; one slim book of poems by Bridges punctuated the flow of classics from the Ashendene Press across forty years. The Hogarth Press stands 'out of series', to use a book catalogue phrase, making pamphlets of lasting importance, farming out longer work to a local printer, becoming a business publisher. Sir Egerton Brydges a century earlier, offering a few efforts of his own and of his son-in-law, followed where taste led him back to the sixteenth and seventeenth centuries; Horace Walpole, except for a re-issue of Gray's *Odes* at Strawberry Hill, printed no poetry. From a literary point of view the only comparison for the Daniel Press would be with Yeats's Cuala Press in Dublin, starting at about the time Daniel finished, but many differences divide them. The Daniel Press never ran as a business, though books were sold; at the Cuala Press they engaged women to work, however poor the wage; it had to achieve some measure of success, with publicity and continuity. In Oxford the scope remained domestic, small books intended for a few. If Cobden-Sanderson got away with calling his product the book beautiful, Daniel might have described his endeavour at Worcester College as the press private.

As a printer Daniel did most of the work himself and in married life his family shared it. If we are to take his childhood hobby half as seriously as Falconer Madan did, he became a printer in 1845 at the age of nine. He died as Provost of Worcester College in 1919.

And we can agree with Madan, because Daniel seems to have been a fortunate child in finding his proper enthusiasm very young. There is true taste, of the kind we connect with his mature printing, in the little pieces from early years at his father's vicarage in Frome. Typographically, there was from the start a Tudor taste about Daniel's printing, as Herbert Warren of Magdalen wrote in his poem:

For you enrich the poet-shrining shelf
    With daintiest treasures old and new, and give,
        In many a nice and justly-ordered page,
Back to mechanic days of haste and pelf
    The tasteful Tudor touch.

A page from a Tudor book, Jaggard's edition of *The Passionate Pilgrim*, 1599, is remarkably similar to Daniel's manner; the sonnet in small type on its small page, with thick bands of type flowers above and below – more flowers than Daniel would have chosen, but the influence is there. And this shows independence from Morris who kept his admiration for German and Italian typography of the fifteenth century. It was the difference between the bias of a designer and a scholar, for both he and Morris shared the two qualities; but design possessed Morris and a taste for Elizabethan poetry remained in Daniel.

It is almost impertinent to write about the Daniel Press, because Madan did so very well – but that was nearly seventy years ago. His remains a flawless bibliography, with some charming essays and poems by friends of the printer. Madan, Bodley's librarian, was a faintly fussy bibliographer, noting the qualities of his own book in Addenda issued later. All is seen in bibliographical terms – the book has a rambling poem in tribute from Masefield, and Madan observes 'the *editio princeps* of a poem by John Masefield has been noted'. Daniel did a Greek exercise in 1857 at Frome, and this is welcomed as 'the only separate edition of the Epistles to the Seven Churches in Greek'. It is an enjoyable bibliography, printed in the Bodleian on Daniel's press in the spirit of Daniel's books. All the little ephemera from Frome and Oxford are faithfully described, and about them he writes with humorous affection:

> Unfortunately there seems to be no dignified and yet suitable term for these waifs and strays, here termed Minor Pieces. One thinks of *leipsana*, Reliquiae, Quisquiliae, Minima, Fragments, Notices, Papers, Scraps, Remanents, Fly-sheets, Broadsides, Fugitive Pieces: but the right word is as elusive as the corresponding one for Magic Lantern. They are what remain when the majestic Car of the professional Cataloguer has passed by and left them strewn on the wayside. The occupant of the Car calls them succinctly and comprehensively Trash.

We see the Daniel Press a little differently now, if only because part of its charm rests with his friends, including Madan, who were writing this book, and with their work, and Oxford of 1880 to 1900.

His books have to be held and read. Sometimes there is no obvious art in the typography – as with *Our Memories*, the fruit of an idea from the eighteen-eighties. Daniel, settled then as a Fellow of Worcester, had the notion that some of his elderly Oxford friends might be persuaded to write short recollections of Oxford as they remembered it fifty and sixty years before; and as they would be recalling famous old characters of that epoch, the essays would evoke ways and people of Oxford in the late eighteenth century. He invited, they accepted; and people who might in those diffident days have feared to write publicly on such personal themes, were happy to do so for the pleasure of a small group. Daniel printed these pieces from time to time as they came to him, and sent them out to friends. They were not for sale. Twenty issues appeared in this way between 1888 and 1893, and two more in 1895 to start a second series which went no further. Sensible readers kept this pleasant gift, and bound it as a book when the time came. No great typographical grace is evident, but an abundance of good tales makes up for that. As Madan puts it, they were 'not ordinary authors, least of all journalists, but Heads of Houses, Canons of Christ Church, and the like, and men who do not write much'.

Most of the Daniel books were planned with immense care. Within their scope one finds small type, flower ornaments, and Mrs Daniel's decorations most delicately executed in red ink on the black page. These might be lightly sketched initial letters, with tendrils curling into the type below, or white letters on a red background, or some beautiful miniated initial showing a meadow and the Oxford skyline. One hundred or a hundred and twenty-five formed the average Daniel Press edition.

A family quality remains in these books time and again. This aspect of the private press is more true here than in any other. May Morris helped a little at Kelmscott, Esther and Lucien Pissarro worked together, but Mrs Daniel and the two girls share in the work or give a purpose to the books. In later years some of the most attractive little books would be set and printed entirely by Mrs Daniel and the children. They tended to use one or other of the small founts – small pica italic as for the *Royal Guest* at Christmas 1900, or brevier roman in the charming little edition of

Ode on the Morning of Christ's Nativity, set up and printed by Mrs Daniel for Christmas 1894. It was quite common since Daniel's boyhood for a book to be prepared at Christmas time, or for a charitable occasion such as a sale of work. Then the early arrivals would be delighted to find copies of a new book from Daniel's press, and the late would regret they had all been sold.

Daniel remains an independent figure, outside fashionable taste and movements, beyond current influences in his printing. His manner was not touched by the common faults for which enterprising printers in his time were criticized; medievalism, escape from the present, or mere scholarship. Sir Basil Blackwell, who made a splendid contribution to private press work, has referred in conversation to 'manufactured rarities'. Daniel Press books are rare for us, because they were made for his friends. Some outsiders treasured these books, and after 1884 he printed for sale but nothing was offered expensively. The published price of Binyon's poems, to take one example, was ten shillings. *Garland of Rachel* was not sold. An indefinable attraction in the Daniel Press might fail if one looked too carefully or tried to analyse.

Though Bridges became so closely connected with the Daniel Press, the books of appreciation which appeared at intervals across six decades since he died, admiring his lyrics, explaining his prosody, interpreting the enormous philosophical poem of his old age, have paid little attention to that small circle of friends whose printed work he gathered about his own at Oxford. In the view of his most recent critic, Donald E. Stanford,* 'He moved in a small circle of carefully selected friends who had artistic and philosophical interests similar to his own. As far as one can make out at this distance, he had no serious faults. One of his few minor weaknesses, however, was a tendency to think too highly of some of his friends' artistic abilities'.

Through the three hundred pages of that book, Daniel is mentioned four times. In Albert Guérard's long critical study of Bridges, published in 1942, he gets one reference.

Counting the five groups of *Shorter Poems* as one, ignoring two brief poems each printed separately, taking two issues of *The Growth of Love* together as a single work, Bridges appeared at

**In the Classic Mode: the Achievement of Robert Bridges*, University of Delaware Press, 1978.

the Daniel Press seven times between 1883 (his play *Prometheus the Firegiver*) and the *Hymns* of 1899. The first Daniel issue of his sonnets *The Growth of Love* was printed anonymously in an edition of only twenty-two copies. Such a connection between poet and printer would seem to deserve more attention than it has received. Yeats supported his family enterprise with patriotic faith at the Cuala Press; quite other motives carried Bridges into the privacy of Daniel's printing.

Though Daniel with that 'tasteful Tudor touch' admired by Warren would print the essays of his Oxford friends, and poetry from the past, over the next quarter century Bridges introduced to this small circle a few whose poems he admired. Presumably Professor Stanford had them in mind, when he mentioned 'a tendency to think too highly of some of his friends' artistic abilities'. As those friends included Hopkins, some of whose poems he wanted Daniel to print, there could be no harm in reading them again; and there are other reasons for returning to the poets Bridges encouraged: Richard Watson Dixon, Henry Patmore (posthumously), Margaret Woods, F.W. Bourdillon, Herbert Warren, Laurence Binyon, Mary Coleridge, Alice Buckton, Ethel Kate Wedgwood.

Victorian England seems to have been especially fertile for the growth of aspiring groups and brotherhoods, intellectual and artistic, lay or monastic. From Pantisocracy to Guilds inspired by Ruskin or Ashbee, schemes of reform by small groups were in the air, often expressing secular aims within the limits of art or socialism. Coleridge, Southey and Wordsworth stopped short at conversation in the Quantocks. While a group known in mockery as the Pre-Raphaelite Brotherhood came together under the influence of Dante Gabriel Rossetti, most of those friends who joined him a few years later in painting the Oxford Union frescoes had been forming their own small brotherhood at King Edward's School, Birmingham, vowed to a monastic future. Among them only Dixon and Fulford entered the church, though Morris and Burne-Jones whom they met at Oxford had also intended as undergraduates to do so. Such aspirations gathered momentum with the heavy addition of *Tracts for the Times*, of Newman and Pusey and Keble, the Oxford Movement, and though not all roads led to Rome one highway pointed there.

It could be interesting to trace such temptations as experienced by young idealists at schools in England, for the movement cannot have existed only at Eton and the relatively minor King Edward's Birmingham. Several passages in the essay about his friend and cousin Digby Dolben who died tragically young show that Bridges, born a decade later than Morris, allied himself with a high-thinking high-church set at Eton. If Dolben, poet and enthusiast, held the banner highest, his letters show some confidence that several among his friends including Bridges, Manning and Cole followed close; that together they would form a new order of Benedictines.

As these spiritual developments affected Bridges we find a logical pattern. Dolben was drowned before going up to Oxford, having failed his entry to Balliol, where Gerard Hopkins was already an undergraduate when Bridges arrived at Corpus. The one occasion when Hopkins met Dolben left such a strong impression that after news of his death Hopkins wrote an emotional tribute bordering upon the excessive. That pattern of acquaintance which for the purpose of this essay led not to Rome but to Daniel's press seems so neat as to have been pre-destined. Hopkins, Anglican at Oxford, was Pater's pupil. At Highgate School his master for a while had been Richard Watson Dixon. Years later as a Jesuit, treasuring the poems which had dropped from their publisher to obscurity, Hopkins wrote to Dixon one of his most charming letters of admiration – the start of their friendship – and introduced him to Bridges.

On the religious front, if Hopkins at Oxford took over where Dolben left off, their combined passions worked otherwise with Bridges who chose the opposite way by becoming a doctor, abandoning as a folly of youth those semi-monastic hopes he had shared with Dolben at Eton, preferring for the rest of his days to forget they had ever concerned him. A philosophy of spiritual joy and visual beauty replaced them.

But a certain withdrawal, fastidiousness, absence of care for wider opinion, stayed with these friends as a heritage from the unworldly ideals they had professed. One might think that in Bridges it was born of disappointment by the small recognition for his *Poems* which Pickering published in 1873, and for the first *Growth of Love* sonnets issued by Bumpus in 1876; yet Bridges had such a habit of secrecy about his writing that in several years of their correspondence Hopkins knew nothing of it, but believed his interest lay in another direction, as a composer. Hopkins for years was adamant that poetry threatened with useless distraction his own path as a Jesuit. Dixon, solitary no less as a curate in

London than in his northern parishes, did suffer disappointment, as we know from letters to Hopkins, from the neglect of his first two published volumes, *Christ's Company* (1861) and *Historic Odes* (1864). His introduction to Daniel by Bridges and Hopkins rescued Dixon from the almost unbearable callousness of one nearby acquaintance in the church to whom he confided each section of his long narrative poem *Mano* as it was completed, only to find at the end that he had never read a word.

1880 is a crucial date, when Edmund Gosse wrote to Daniel suggesting Bridges as a contributor to *The Garland of Rachel*. Either as a result of serious illness at that time, or from a longer scheme of life which would have been characteristic of him, or the coincidence of both, Bridges withdrew from medicine and London to live with his mother, for the second time a widow, at Yattendon where a couple of years later he married Monica Waterhouse. Even before cars afflicted those roads, Yattendon was within simple range of Oxford.

The prospect that Daniel's press might provide for his poems and those of his friends that peace which the world seemed unable to give must then have struck him; for in 1881 came the suggestion of a composite volume which would have included all three of them and thus changed the history of English literature. Between 1883 and 1890 Daniel was printing in small editions five volumes by Bridges, three by Dixon, one by Henry Patmore. Margaret Woods and F. W. Bourdillon also appear in those years.

Bridges soared highest as lyric poet (which is where his reputation lay until he achieved new fame in 1929 with *The Testament of Beauty*) during Daniel's most productive period, the last two decades of the nineteenth century. 1890 has slight significance as ending Dixon's connection with the Press, though he lived on with reduced powers until 1900 and several of the poems published posthumously were among his finest; and in 1891 Morris produced the first Kelmscott Press book, giving to private presses a fashionable air which Bridges in his withdrawal preferred to avoid.

Daniel's press followed its Oxford ways; no influence from these London ventures altered him. Perhaps through the mutual friendship of Horace Hart, Printer to the University, advising them both as to type, making those Oxford founts available, Ashendene books of the nineties look like Daniel's. Hornby and the Daniels exchanged their latest productions, with warm letters of thanks. Both printers at that time were their own compositors, unlike Morris or Ricketts or, later, Cobden-Sanderson and Walker. In that correspondence Mrs Daniel's dreams of some mighty edition never approached reality; Oxford life was too busy, with all its distractions, and they had not the means.

Bridges in 1897 thanked Hornby for the gift of an Ashendene book, sent at the suggestion of Daniel in whose house he had admired it. 'I am very glad indeed that you use old type' Bridges wrote, 'the new imitations of it of Morris and others seem to miss its beauty altogether, & tho' 'Fell' is not the best that ever was, it is better than the imitation of the very best'. And this curiously prophetic letter continues with a hope that 'some day you will get a true reproduction of one of the great Italian founts'.

Bridges preserved, at Yattendon and on Boar's Hill, a marvellous detachment conducive to unconventional views upon literature and print. That wish he expressed to Hornby, probably not father to the thought in this instance, was fulfilled to the letter. Who but he and Hopkins in their remoteness could express critical distaste for Shakespeare's vulgarity, publicly as Bridges did in an essay, or privately as when Hopkins deplored passages 'suggestive of horn-jokes, Benedicks, and all that kind of thing, tedious when not odious'*?

Then from Worcester College in the 1890s came a volume of Binyon's poems, natural fruit of residence at Trinity and his evening with Bridges at the Woods' cottage on Boar's Hill; a second book of poems by Margaret Woods; the five parts, plus index, of Bridges' *Shorter Poems*, his best known collection as lyric poet; and one addition of absorbing interest, a slender octavo in paper covers called *Fancy's Following*, by 'Anodos'. The author was Mary Coleridge, whose genius elevates the Daniel Press and whose perceptive friendship with Dixon completed that quartet which provided its highest qualities. Of Dixon's wonderful *Last Poems* published in 1905 without even the appreciation of his admirers Mary Coleridge wrote, 'They are quiet; they make no stir; they are full of secret beauty that will not unfold itself excepting to the touch of love and reverence'.

Her judgement of Dixon's small volume may stand for my theme, the poets of the Daniel Press. In a quest for beauty, avoiding emotional excess, they argued in lengthy letters the details of prosody. Stress, quantity, speech rhythm, sprung rhythm, any reader now may find it hard to understand their definitions. In-

*April 1879, Hopkins to Bridges.

stinct would not serve, training in the classics made rules a necessity. After designing his alphabets Dürer had found a similar desire to justify himself in complex schemes of geometry. Recalling the years at Eton in his own essay on Dolben, Bridges had written: 'What had led me to poetry was the inexhaustible satisfaction of form, the magic of speech, lying as it seemed to me in the masterly control of the material: it was an art which I hoped to learn'.

Anyone may find himself absorbed as confused in reading the letters of these poets about their art, and later critics confound our muddle. Of the metre in *Testament of Beauty* Nowell Charles Smith described the normal line as having twelve syllables and six stresses; Guérard contradicted him, writing that most lines 'have twelve syllables and a completely indeterminate number of stresses or accents'. Yvor Winters believed the lines have five stresses, a relief to me for that was my natural habit in reading the whole poem aloud. Winters also thought Bridges in his infinite analysis of Milton's prosody misunderstood that subject which tended to dominate such discussions with Hopkins.

Varied quantity needs no explaining, varied stress is manifest in all Shakespeare's complex passages, in such lines as:

> Time hath my lord a wallet at his back
> Wherein to place alms for oblivion,
> A great-sized monster of ingratitude.

which nobody could be guilty of reading as iambic pentameter. Hopkins, with a double first in Greats at Oxford, chose to find rules for his eccentricities while claiming that if read aloud the poetry became comprehensible by rhythm of common speech.

If they preferred argument about prosody to that 'immense range of human experience' which John Sparrow finds lacking in Bridges, we may look again at Binyon writing nearly half a century ago to recall a vitality in the theme which is lost to us now: 'The younger generation of today can, I think, have no conception of the angry passions and resentment caused among critics of that day by any liberties taken with traditional metre'. It would have been congenial talk at Worcester College and on Boar's Hill, acceptable within small scope at the Daniel Press.

Bridges and Hopkins chose a remoteness which both could have found unbearable but for the exchanges of letters among those few who cared to understand: Patmore, a popular poet, came into the circle, and Dixon who had remoteness thrust upon him. They strove with none for none was worth their strife – and Landor's second sentiment could also apply: nature they loved and next to nature art.

Yet they believed these tools of the new prosody, forged in private, would create great verse of the future; they were the modern poets working without noise, a small elite in small editions.

ROBERT BRIDGES

Such varied critical views characterise the many books about Bridges, that we approach him across open territory. Reticent for the first decades of adult life, his reputation grew as lyric poet and author of a sonnet sequence, *The Growth of Love*. Never a teaching member of the University, after retiring from his medical career he lived near Oxford, at Yattendon and after 1907 on Boar's Hill. His competence in the classics and the history of English prosody would have merited an Oxford Fellowship but he chose to live above Oxford; he took pleasure in descending to it.

He was gruff and obstinate in argument, nursing an independence which sprang from privacy of means and temperament. A different mood appears in three affectionate essays he wrote at intervals after the deaths of his friends, Dolben, Dixon and Bradley; the task of writing a comparable memoir about the fourth and most famous friend, Hopkins, defeated him. If the serious conflict in religious attitudes which threatened their intimacy puzzles us now, a moment of endearing confession redeems him in the Bradley essay, where Bridges wrote:

> It was after his death that one of his daughters told me that the family did not altogether like his going to church with them, because he was liable on occasion to disturb their decorum by a sudden access of laughter during the service. I welcomed this disclosure, since it is the very complaint that my own family make against me; and my discredit is mitigated by the partnership of one whose genuine piety and reverence were unquestionable.

These two old bearded men from Victorian England, what did they laugh at in church, unknown to each other? Bridges cherished his Anglican connection through vicissitudes of High Church aspiration and scientific knowledge, happy in the prospect of meeting old friends after death 'difficult as it is with our sorrowful experience to face with any comfort the prospect of a general resurrection'. The crowds would have appalled him.

A series of withdrawals formed his pattern of life; from Dolben's aspirations, from medicine, from publication, from London;

until in the last years the fruit of his life, an enormous philosophical poem arriving unheralded, achieved the public success nobody expected. Without making enemies, independence was the essence of his story. A rare power of character sustained his pursuit of a poet's way; in fallow period she could follow his absorptions as essayist or moving spirit in the Society for Pure English, much concerned to devise rational spelling and establish the new prosody of varied stress he had so often discussed in correspondence with Hopkins and Patmore. Living for his art, nobody so despised fashion. As a perceptive critic he is impressive now, especially when he wrote about the work of a friend. Though he disliked obscurity, if that seemed unavoidable to express the poet's concept he would define and imaginatively explain it.

Whatever the oddities of his discomfort as he presented Hopkins to the world, deep affection is assumed in the critical notes; he was not damning with faint praise. As to Dixon and Mary Coleridge, public neglect had no influence upon his judgement, convinced of a comparison with Blake.

In his art, which formed most of what he cared for, the stance of Bridges was revolutionary. It is easy to remember him as conservative, against the new poetry, because several ideas for which he fought are in eclipse. Except a couple of lyrics common in anthologies, few read his poems; nobody notices the orthography he advocated, the Society for Pure English might as well not have existed. Beauty as a concept among poets lies beyond the pale. Bridges is mistrusted for commending the genius of forgotten authors, and blamed either for holding back Hopkins too long or introducing grudgingly. His own metrical experiments, cherished and academic, receive no attention while the 'sprung rhythm' of Hopkins has been endlessly discussed. If ever poet invented a good public phrase, it was 'sprung rhythm'. Neither poet nor critic through a century has comprehended it or succeeded in establishing a definition. Why sprung, one still asks, why rhythm?

So Bridges has been unfortunate publicly since he died, but that would not have worried his spirit, confident his time will come. Smaller figures pass, fashionably exalted. Perhaps the good sense of his orthography will appear, as use of English spreads; those brought up in other languages would find it helpful to know that it struck him as absurd in childhood that C A T meant cat, when to him it clearly spelt sate – and so through the distinctions between *that* and *thatt* as he wanted them said or read, *have* and *hav*, in poetic values which remain the domain of unreliable instinct.

Bridges as sympathetic critic wrote a marvellous essay in appreciation of Mary Coleridge, which appeared in *The Cornhill* a few weeks after her death in 1907. Thus he recorded in memorable essays his understanding of the two poets he introduced to the Daniel Press, and those other two he had wished to bring into a composite volume: Dolben, Dixon, Hopkins, Mary Coleridge. It is specious but excusable to remember them all in this recollection of Daniel Press poets.

His part in designing his books has been analysed by Nicolas Barker and, most recently, Donald Stanford whose serious critical work continues to bring Bridges back into academic orbit. It would be absurd to suggest of any writer that he was indifferent to public opinion, but Bridges came close as anyone to that modest detachment. The safeties, it may be suggested, mattered more to him: security of that foundation in the classics, ever alive to him and a few friends but disappearing from the culture of his time; safe without need to worry about sales or royalties; safely away in Yattendon or on the hill above Oxford, member of no committee, owing no service to powerful groups except the strong patriotism which came to him by temperament; secure in his friendship to follow that mental speculation which he described in a longish and delightful poem, shadowing *The Testament of Beauty*, printed by Daniel in 1903, and even more thoroughly neglected now than most of the rest of Bridges, *Now in Wintry Delights*.

Born in a fair place which overlooked the sea, an early memory was of Napier's expedition sailing through the English Channel for the Baltic. The Duke of Wellington as Warden of the Cinque Ports had a house not far away. His descriptive memories in such a poem as 'Who has not walked upon the shore . . .' with the lovely verse about clouds,

> From distant hills their shadows creep,
> Arrive in turn and mount the lea,
> And flit across the down, and leap
> Sheer off the cliff upon the sea

are from childhood there; for he went to Eton at the age of ten, soon after his father's death. A year later his mother married the Vicar of Rochdale in Lancashire. There is no hint of her future happiness or otherwise, but Bridges never wrote about his new home in the north.

Eton he enjoyed to a degree which is unconventional among

poets, finding friends, rowing, passing easily to Corpus Christi College at Oxford which was not the most natural place for an Etonian. 'The Curfew Tower', a poem in the slim volume printed for him at the Ashendene Press in 1915, expresses his affection for the Eton environment. Another from that same group, 'Fly-catchers', may well have belonged to Eton – I have not come upon evidence, as has sometimes been said, that it refers to some school he attended earlier (if indeed he did) at Walmer. Less than affectionate or flattering, he recalls a dreary schoolmaster 'sixty summers ago', which would have been when he first went to Eton, who almost killed his 'eager and hungry' enthusiasm,

> Stood over us and from a desk fed us with flies.
> Dead flies – such as litter the library south-window,
> That buzzed at the panes until they fell stiff-baked on the sill,
> Or are roll'd up asleep i' the blinds at sunrise,
> Or wafer'd flat in a shrunken folio.
> A dry biped he was, nurtured likewise
> On skins and skeletons, stale from top to toe
> With all manner of rubbish & all manner of lies.

His love of literature and the classics survived it well.

In his memoir of Dolben, Bridges drops hints more openly than elsewhere about his own religious leanings at Eton. Their friendship took an unexpected course, for Digby Mackworth Dolben was a distant cousin and Bridges had the unwelcome duty there of keeping a protective eye on him. They became intimate, to use the pre-Freudian phrase for simple friendship, so far that Dolben's eccentricities of thought and conduct swept his older cousin towards sharing his religious aspirations. That Bridges at Eton became one of a small circle of high-church enthusiasts emerges beyond doubt from that essay.

> A sectarian training had provided us with premises, which, so long as they remained unquestioned, were of overwhelming significance: they dominated everything: the logical situation was appalling: the ordinary conventions of life were to us merely absurd: we regarded the claim of the church in the same way as Cardinal Newman had elaborated it in his writings; and we were no doubt directly influenced by his views, though I had never myself read any conventional books, and had little taste for them. We were in fact both of us Pusey-ites, and if we

reacted somewhat differently to the same influences, yet neither of us at that time doubted that our *toga virilis* would be the cassock of a priest or the habit of a monk.

Bridges half a century later wrote with amusing diffidence about all this, no doubt genuinely forgetting how he had become involved in something he so thoroughly abandoned. Dolben's wild charm carried that day. It was to be, he recalls, 'a Brotherhood, or the scheme of a Brotherhood, among himself and his friends. . . . It was I suppose, the same sort of idea that had grown up between Wm. Morris and his friends, ten years earlier, at Oxford'. Dolben was the moving spirit: 'He, who was to decide everything, and I, who was to be the head of the community, could never of course disagree with him'.

However Bridges remembered it as Poet Laureate, he must have travelled some distance along that road for Dolben to have appointed him head of the future community, and his simple statement is there, 'We were in fact both of us Pusey-ites'.

Though Dolben's death ended that episode, Gerard Manley Hopkins took over as hound of heaven. Bridges' rejection of orthodox religion, his decision to become a doctor, is an intriguing turn in his life's pattern. Against the intellectual background of that moment, one decision looks like a branch of the other. At St Bartholomew's Hospital he was house physician, then casualty physician, and in 1878 became assistant physician at the children's hospital in Great Ormond Street. Thus he made a practical entry into the world of real help.

So Bridges, opposed to parlour socialism, served his apprenticeship to human suffering. That was his reply, though he would never have put it thus, to Dolben and Hopkins. In the essay on Dolben he mentions that at Oxford he was 'drifting fast away from our old religious sympathies in a different direction from him'. When Hopkins, declaring his own sympathy with communism, suggested Bridges give away money charitably to the point of inconvenience the advice was much resented. 'I take leave to repeat and you cannot but see', he had written, 'that it is a noble thing and not a miserable something or other to give alms and help the needy and stint ourselves for the sake of the unhappy or deserving'.

Their correspondence ceased for several years after this exposure of a raw nerve. Such a dilemma had afflicted others. Morris and Bridges had this in common, the practical knowledge of misery opposed to conditions in which they could work as artists. If it appears that Bridges travelled too far from the hospitals in seeking poetic tranquillity, he could look back to a form of national service nobody forced upon him. The trauma of those years is only known to us in one famous poem, 'On a Dead Child'. Perhaps his anti-socialist passage in *The Testament of Beuaty* is a late reply from old conscience to Hopkins – but nobody can insist that Bridges ought to have been a socialist.

Once withdrawn, the further retreat came easily. Prosody not medicine occupied his brain, philosophy of science rather than the casualty ward. Aloof from the committee life in which Oxford must ever have involved Fellows of Colleges, academic detail absorbed him in establishing different verse forms or, as diversion from that, making for poets a new orthography. As critic and in the way he spent the time Bridges dared to be original; and growing older, opposition was often dismissed conversationally as nonsense. There seemed no need to take much note of other points of view. Since literary decorum struck him as a necessary point of breeding, he deplored Shakespeare's coarseness. The point of view would not commend itself to present-day directors at Stratford. When Gosse edited Webster's play *Love's Graduate* for Daniel's press in 1885, they all agreed it began life as two plays, a vulgar plot grafted by some other hand upon Webster's refinement; so Gosse performed his surgery, and the decent version was printed. Bridges became a strong imperialist, as did Hopkins who lamented in April 1881 that 'We have been shamefully beaten by the Boers (at Majuba it was simply that our troops funked and ran) . . .' and fumed a couple of months later that 'the Transvaal is an unredeemed disgrace. And people do not seem to mind. You know that our troops ('our gallant fellows', as the reporter had it) ran'.

Fashionless withdrawal characterises the structure and mood of Bridges' lyric poems. Francis Brett Young, in the book dismissed by heavier critics as a lightweight laureate tribute, had interesting passages on the use of conventional epithet in many of the *Shorter Poems*. 'It is one of the signs, I think, of the great poet', he wrote, 'that he is fearless in using the obvious epithet where it will serve a coherent picture, as it is of the small one that, in these very conditions, he abandons it to grope for the exalting phrase'. And again, 'He gives us none of the false currency of fine phrases'.

The expected adjective seems at first to place Bridges among a host of Victorian-Homeric poets, as does his use of outdated word forms; but to them one can apply such an apologia as he gave in the 'Publisher's Note' tipped into the final pages of *Testament of Beauty*. At the end of that note 'the author would explain that the use of *-eth* for the 3rd per. sing. of verbs is not an archaic fancy, but a practical advantage, indispensable to him, not only for its syllabic lightness, but because by distinguishing verbs from the identical substantives, it sharpens the rhetoric and often liberates the syntax'.

Written in the late nineteen-twenties, that defence suggests he had been subject to some criticism and felt he had the right to reply. Half a century earlier, no such explanation was needed. Colloquial English became customary among between-the-wars poets, as it had been for Browning. I remember a schoolmaster telling us to 'avoid the 'tises and 'twases'. Bridges and Hopkins so far from ignoring common speech in their poetry, interested themselves in another aspect, its stress and rhythm. We may read much about the technical perfection of Bridges' lyric poems and his sonnets; if we accept first that his effects were well known to him and intentional, our approach becomes simpler.

One other device used commonly by him and his friends, abandoned at certain levels since, is the conceit – as in this stanza, from a poem admired once, 'Nightingales':

> Nay, barren are those mountains and spent the streams:
> Our song is the voice of desire, that haunts our dreams,
>   A throe of the heart,
> Whose pining visions dim, forbidden hopes profound,
> No dying cadence nor long sigh can sound,
>   For all our art.

It has all that a first taste of Bridges would reject – unfairly quoted here, out of context, the middle verse of three. 'Nay', at least three inversions, no verb or adjective unexpected. Those points have already been mentioned, but the poem's conceit remains: why should a poet suppose, we ask with literal mind, that bird-song expresses some ecstatic longing for fine scenery in 'the mountains whence ye come?'. Do birds admire mountain contours? And have the nightingales heard Bridges so clearly that they reply in those lines quoted above, declaring they came from a dreary place and vainly sing for unattainable ideals? Is it a lot of nonsense, from which poets in our day have mercifully withdrawn?

Second and third readings reveal the conceit as allegory, though we may dismiss at first sight as out-of-taste the apparently simple verses in Bridges. 'Nightingales' is not the dream of a simpleton: Bridges uses the device as allegory for his own apparently blissful poems, or even for the condition of all poets who seem to pour forth songs of praise beneath which the deeper sadness exists. Dixon's deceptively simple lyrics, 'Fallen Rain' and 'The Feathers of the Willow' may be understood in the same spirit.

Conventional epithet, apparent simplicity, both were facets of reticence. As to privacy in prosody, one may judge that the correspondence between Hopkins, Bridges, Patmore and Dixon assumed the character of a small club, exclusive because excluding: they were by no means reticent, but choice and master spirits of that age fashioning the next century's poetry. Their mutual fondness for Purcell, evident in a Hopkins sonnet and a stanza in *Eros and Psyche* where Bridges spells his name in the first letters of each line, displayed a musical taste removed from current sentiment. But the poetic effect in these several friends was the same: 'In fact', Hopkins had written to Bridges in 1866, 'it occurs to me that you are unusually reticent and certainly have a great respect for reticence'. It will take a very vigilant thesis-writer to unravel the anonymity of *The Growth of Love*. There is a touching cry in sonnet 58 from that sequence which Daniel twice printed:

> O my uncared-for songs, what are ye worth,
> That in my secret book with so much care
> I write you, this one here and that one there,
> Marking the time and order of your birth?
> How, with a fancy so unkind to mirth,
> A sense so hard, a style so worn and bare,
> Look ye for any welcome anywhere
> From any shelf or heart-home on the earth?

There cannot have been a poet in the aristocratic history of manuscript whose reticence meant total exclusion 'from any shelf or heart-home on the earth'.

His ideal, as anyone agrees without needing the title of his last long poem, was beauty. Bridges must have known that no towers of purer ivory existed than his at Yattendon and the house he called Chilswell on Boar's Hill. An attraction in reading him now is acquaintance with the last great Victorian; for he made no attempt as Morris had to escape his period, but accepted traditional diction and became fascinated by its science. His detachment was philosophic. It is not impossible, though it may be impertinent, to question John Sparrow's verdict that 'a devotion to Beauty in Bridges's sense cuts off the poet from an immense range of human experience; and this was a sacrifice that Bridges was very ready to make in the interests of his art'.

Hopkins went further in his creed of beauty, believing that 'for work to be perfect there ought to be the sense of beauty in the highest degree both in the artist and in the age, the style and keepings of which the artist employs'. In that regard he found Renaissance Italy and its artists imperfect.

Though the letters from Bridges do not survive, we receive one vital clue from Hopkins in a letter he wrote in 1881: 'What you say about the run of people not liking nor knowing what to make of your writing and this giving you satisfaction opens out a wide vein of to me saddening thoughts which I shall not now enter on'.

There is an impressive line in a play by Arthur Miller, of forgiveness with regard to the central character, 'For he allowed himself to be wholly known'. One can appreciate – in the *Growth of Love* passage quoted above for instance – that Bridges would like to have been 'wholly known' but not misunderstood. Daniel offered the 'little clan' for whom Keats left great verse. It is a coincidence that of all popular romantic poets only Keats was printed at the Daniel Press.

A strong aesthetic interest shown by Bridges in the production of all his books overlay a bibliophile fear of disappointment if a volume were opened. These are matters almost inexplicable to those who do not share this strange attitude to books. A parallel exists between a collector's fear of disappointment in reading or opening what he loves to possess, and the poet's fear of being read with imperfect sympathy. Both are perfectionists. The sensitivity would perhaps be more painful when, as in Bridges, the poem has been perfected to a kind of simplicity which could easily be misunderstood. Each of the two, poet and reader, fears the plunder of a beautiful object.

We are back in the theme of privacy which Hopkins perversely disapproved. 'He tried', as Professor Ritz put it, 'to laugh him out of a course of conduct that was prejudicial to his future renown'. In the last year of his life Hopkins teased Bridges on this point, referring to the first, anonymous Daniel Press edition of *The Growth of Love*:

> For consider: you aim at oblivion; for that you descend into Daniel's den; for that you print 24 copies* (so that the College of Apostles on parting could have taken two copies only for the needs of all Scythia, suppose, all Parthia, all India, and so on). Now . . . you can be forgotten 'as hard' at Dublin as anywhere else, at Lampsacus as at Clazomenae: what do you want more?

Bridges perhaps did not descend into Daniel's den aiming at oblivion, but fearing exposure. Patmore also complained that he 'professes to feel a profound indifference as to whether people read his poems or not. I cannot understand this'.†

We may find the map of Bridges' independence in the Dolben essay, and many of his poems. About Ruskin he felt as some may in our own time towards advice as to architectural taste in Pevsner, unable to 'imagine how another person could presume to tell me what I should like or dislike'. Though never following the private habits of Dolben who 'crossed himself at meals, and left his queer books about, and behaved generally so as to make himself and his opinions a ridiculous wonder to the boys', he seems at least to have given the impression of willingness to join Dolben's 'Third Order of S. Benedict'. 'He seemed inclined to join it', Dolben told Coles.

As absolute solitude looks unbearable, Brotherhoods became the refuge in that period of high religious thought. Hopkins in the Jesuit discipline took an absurd though charitable stance in chiding the others for their withdrawal. The Daniel Press has a special position as the last shadow of Victorian Brotherhoods, for there is a distinction between it and the reformers who attempted a different ideal in Guild Socialism. Ashbee with his Guild of Handicraft, the kibbutzim in Israel, ashrams in California, a wilderness of such gardens has continued but fastidious privacy was not a feature in their design.

When Bridges had so far departed from the self-denial Hopkins adopted, as to let advice about charitably giving a fair portion of his wealth interrupt their exchange of letters for three years, 'I think, my dear Bridges', Hopkins reasonably wrote, 'to be so much offended about that red letter was excessive'.

When Bridges became expansive on the theme of socialism, none more conscious than he of the relative injustice which com-

*In fact he printed 22.

†Quoted by Ritz. p. 110.

fortable circumstances implied, a kind of diffident humour entered his writing. Two long ruminations in which he faced and discussed what would now be called his life-style are almost hidden under the title *Poems in Classical Prosody*, as if these were technical exercises not to be swallowed as philosophy. Defending a degree of indulgence, too public a statement could seem tasteless. The title is another form of withdrawal; it happens that one of them, 'Now in Wintry Delights' was printed by Daniel and the other, 'To a Socialist in London', he wrote after the Daniel Press had closed. Both deserve to be better known for what they say; we are not to be deceived by that title into by-passing them as metrical experiments leading to *The Testament of Beauty*. In the second of the two he asks Fraser to whom it is written, author of *The Golden Bough*, to accept that he is aware of suffering: 'Spare me the story; believe more feel this grief than avow it'.

If spared the story, and the deprivation Socialists of Fraser's persuasion would order, he could still enjoy the emblems of affluent privacy on Boar's Hill:

> My Japanese paintings, my fair blue Cheney, Hellenic
> Statues and Caroline Silver, my beautiful Aldines,
> Prized so highly because so few, so fondly familiar,
> Need no tongue to defend them against rude hands, that assail
> them
> Only because their name is RARITY; hands insensate,
> Rending away pitilessly the fair embroideries of life,
> That close-clust'ring man, his comfort pared to the outskirts
> Of his discomfort, may share in meanness unenvied.

Guérard believed these intimate *Classical Prosody* experiments caused 'some of the ugliest lines in English poetry', offering as instances: 'In the flat accretions of new sedimentary strata' and 'her metamorphoses transmuting by correlation . . .' But a merit of the method, which we find also in Eliot's plays, is the ease of rise and fall from conversation to poetic flight, evocative overtone to pure prose – and with Bridges, to the indulgent use of abstraction by which his philosophy was exposed. He developed this habit more fully in *The Testament of Beauty*. In the *Classical Prosody* poems it came with playful originality, Bridges in a quiet corner enjoying himself with new freedom.

His concern was not in the merit of such freedom, but its control which seemed to call for the discipline of rules. In letters to Hopkins and the several editions of his long essay on Milton's prosody this need for confinement, some border to the new territory, absorbed him. If Milton was untroubled by the need for such extensive apologia, perhaps it was because his estate already had clear boundaries.

It is easy to see a connection, the same mind at work, between Bridges on prosody and on phonetic spelling. Of his Milton findings he had written in 1901, 'These "laws" are merely the tabulation of what my ear finds in English stressed or accentual verse: but they appeal confidently to the reader's ear for confirmation'. The zeal for phonetic reform, an instance of unbroken development in the pattern of Bridges' long life, went back to his nursery.

A friend Bridges and Hopkins tried to co-opt for their scheme of prosody was Coventry Patmore who had written about metre in the preface to his poem 'Amelia'. Patmore's odes in irregular stress and line length brought him within the circle of their friendship but he was older, less ready to think it out again; no statement of the sort they wanted came from him. 'The interest which you take in the grammar of English verse has led me to hope that you would not be disinclined to give an account in print of what Hopkins and I call the new prosody'–the suggestion came from Yattendon in September 1883.* And Alice Meynell's introduction to the catalogue of Patmore's library makes it clear he had thought on the same wave length: 'The lines and pauses of the Odes measured chiefly by the variable breathing of thought and passion, he holds to be the work of an art all his own, even his own discovery. Let it be noted that when he talked of his poems, it was of their metres'.

In the particular matter of rules this is not the place to consider Hopkins, who was not after all a Daniel poet, but the balance of his attitude was expressed in a letter to Bridges, August 1877, where he claims 'my apparent licences are counterbalanced, and more, by my strictness'.

Bridges wrote eight verse plays, of which Guérard (a pupil of Yvor Winters) believed 'The indifference in which Bridges' plays are held can be explained only by the fact that almost no one has read them'. Winters wrote in the highest terms of the two *Nero* plays,

*Quoted by Derek Patmore, p. 191.

> ... one of the most remarkable narrative works that I know ... for the most part it is compact and effective speech, modulated and clarified by the subtleties of a blank verse which is the work of a master and which is not in any way Elizabethan or Victorian ... The work was first published late in the nineteenth century, but it seems to have been written with the twentieth century in mind ... it is a great work that almost no one has read ...

Brett Young on the same play:

> Of *Nero*, which is published in two parts, and was begun and finished at very different stages of Bridges' craftsmanship, one is forced to admit that it has most of the failings of the other dramatic work, and is redeemed by less than the usual amount of poetry.

Of the Masks, Odes and Dramas John Sparrow judged 'we feel that we are reading a poetical exercise'.

On such evidence Bridges could be called a controversial poet, but the world forgets him. A recent verbal verdict was 'surely some schoolgirls know a bit of his work'. *Prometheus the Firegiver* and *The Feast of Bacchus* as Daniel Press plays fall within the scope of this essay. Hopkins told Bridges of *Prometheus*,* 'how beautiful and masterly it is, what a sense of style, unknown in our age, in the phrasing and the verse, how vigorous the thought, and how Greek, whether you wished it or not, the choruses, and yet so fresh'.

It would be absurd here to travel through Hopkins' letters to Bridges, of which we have only one side and must reconstruct the other. It was not an easy friendship, nor built upon simple admiration. One moment of insight is public, after Bridges had received the manuscript of *The Wreck of the Deutschland* and made some insensitive reply, when Hopkins writes: 'You say you wd. not for any money read my poem again. Nevertheless I beg you will. Besides money, you know, there is love'.†

A few months later he writes 'I must tell you I am sorry you never read the Deutschland again'.

Charity and authority inform Hopkins' letters and it seems doubtful that a comparable provision of either came in return.

*June 1882. †August 1877.

Neither was free of a quality near to jealousy or envy, which in Hopkins appears in such sentences as this,* of an especially successful poem: 'The *Passer By* in particular reads not so much like sprung rhythm as that logaoedic dignified-doggrel one Tennyson has employed in *Maud* and since.' In October 1880 he dares criticize that wholly successful poem 'London Snow', and 'On a Dead Child', in terms which now look both false and graceless. The minor changes he suggested in 'London Snow' ('a most beautiful and successful piece', he allows) were not adopted. His proposal is foolish and pedantic that in the snowy soft line 'Difference hiding, making unevenness even', the phrase should be altered to 'making uneven even' 'since "unevenness", in which the *n* is really doubled, is an awkward word'. And 'The rhythm, as I told you, is not quite perfect. That of the child-piece is worse, indeed *it is* Browningese, if you like . . . You are certainly less at your ease in sprung rhythm'.

Nobody knows why the letters to Hopkins were destroyed; part of the reticence, it is usually suggested, a facet of his defence against biography. One extraordinary passage is quoted by Ritz, in considering why Bridges delayed so long before publishing the poems, from a letter Bridges wrote to Hopkins' mother in 1890:

> I should myself prefer the postponement of the poems till the memoir is written, *or* till I have got my own method of prosody recognised separately from Gerard's. They are the same, and he has the greater claim than I do to the origination of it, but he has used it so as to discredit it: and it would be a bad start in favour for the practice we both advocated and wished to be used.

And nobody knows why the memoir was never written. Deep differences in taste, religious and poetic, must have played their part in a private censorship. It seems unforgivably short-sighted of Bridges, though understandable in the code of his day, to have deprived us of such a book as he could have written. Instead we have his long *Preface to the Notes* with its apology for 'Mannerism', 'Style', 'Oddity', 'Obscurity' in Hopkins.

Without quoting to excess now, a summary of Bridges' consideration of Hopkins appears in two moments of progression from his letters to Patmore. At first† he is introducing the poems, which

*February 1879. †September 1883.

> . . . are quite unique; and tho' their eccentricities will always prevent their being in any sense popular their extraordinary poetical qualities will preserve them as long as artistic feeling remains in literature . . . The interest which you take in the grammar of English verse has led me to hope that you would not be disinclined to give an account in print of what Hopkins and I call the new prosody.

Patmore will receive them, he agrees in a reply two months later. Such correspondence tended to be slow in its enthusiasm. In December Bridges becomes nervous to the point of uncharity that their new prosody may be judged by Hopkins' practice:

> But lest you should be ill-prepared for these poems I should tell you that Gerard Hopkins is affected in style. His affectation is somewhat natural to him, however, and subservient to general effect. I should say it was artistically used, tho' not always pleasant. I think of him, as of Dixon, that he must always be treasured by poetic minds on account of his original beauties. I hope you will think so – I feel foolish in writing confidential wisdom concerning my betters.
>
> As to the prosody which should be the subject of this letter, H. pushes it to its extreme limits. If there is an *ad absurdum* of it he exhibits it. He has (for instance) in my opinion, an absolutely wrong notion of rhyme. He does not consider that it makes necessarily any pause in the rhythm. This would affect his rhythm to my ears unfavourably in whatsoever prosody he wrote, and you will exclude the effect produced by it from the proper effect of the prosody. Then you will see that he is naturally bent towards subtlety of rhythm as well as of expression, and you will have another allowance to make there, and judge where the prosody seems unintelligible at first reading (if it should seem so) that he is playing some trick on it. – His music, for he has written some airs, would give an excellent example of the way in which he loves to elaborate the simplest forms.
>
> The results of all these qualities is a 'product' which is unique. I do not suppose that there is anything like him in the world. Tho' there is much in his poems which I should not defend as *useful* prosody, yet you will find plenty of passages where the full force of the system, his originality, which I advocate, is well shown.

A touching paradox in Bridges whose life and poetry explored classic territory was his fondness for such unexpected characters as Hopkins, Dixon, Dolben and Mary Coleridge. From his several essays about them, and the 1918 notes to Hopkins' poems, there is no doubt that the eccentricity of these friends appealed to him: Dolben's wild schemes and habits at Eton, Dixon's melancholy solitude mingling with a passion for garden tennis, Mary Coleridge more strictly as a poet in the subtle essay on her work; and in the Hopkins notes when he writes about 'all the rude shocks of his purely artistic wantonness' we realise his phrases are affectionate. As records in friendship the memoirs of Dolben and Dixon hold their appeal. Bridges wanted to bring them all into the quiet life of Daniel's press.

After a serious short contribution for *The Garland of Rachel*, 1881, his first Daniel Press book, *Prometheus the Firegiver*, issued in July 1883, has near the end a characteristic passage which forms the better version of the poem 'O my vague desires' which would appear with additional lines in his Daniel volume of poems a year later. As often with Bridges, one has to avoid the temptation of dismissing at first sight. What are his desires, 'For ever soaring aloft, soaring and dying', the poet's dissatisfactions? His perennial answer is 'Joy, the joy of flight'. He was the poet of joy, beauty, indefinable.

O my vague desires!
Ye lambent flames of the soul, her offspring fires:
That are my soul herself in pangs sublime
Rising and flying to heaven before her time:
What doth tempt you forth
To melt in the south or shiver in the frosty north?
What seek ye or find ye in your random flying,
For ever soaring aloft, soaring and dying?
Joy, the joy of flight;
They hide in the sun, they flare and dance in the night.
Gone up, gone out of sight – and ever again
Follow fresh tongues of fire, fresh pangs of pain.
Ah! could I control
These vague desires, these leaping flames of the soul:
Could I but quench the fire, ah! could I stay
My soul that flieth, alas, and dieth away!

Though a principle in choosing these few poems by way of illustration will be that they were first printed by Daniel, 'London Snow' from the 1884 Daniel Press *Poems* is an exception; well known, not only perfect as word-painting but showing that Bridges could very well manage without using archaic word-forms. He and Hopkins may have viewed it in the first instance as an experiment in the rhythm of stress. All of the 1884 collection would be reprinted by Daniel in *Shorter Poems*, with a fifth section which was new. By 1884 the first three sections had already appeared, the fourth was new. 'London Snow' had then no title, except its first phrase 'When men were all asleep'.

When men were all asleep the snow came flying,
In large white flakes falling on the city brown,
Stealthily and perpetually settling and loosely lying,
  Hushing the latest traffic of the drowsy town;
Deadening, muffling, stifling its murmurs failing;
Lazily and incessantly floating down and down:
  Silently sifting and veiling road, roof and railing;
Hiding difference, making unevenness even,
Into angles and crevices softly drifting and sailing.
  All night it fell, and when full inches seven
It lay in the depth of its uncompacted lightness,
Its clouds blew off from a high and frosty heaven;
  And all woke earlier for the unaccustomed brightness
Of the winter dawning, the strange unheavenly glare:
The eye marvelled – marvelled at the dazzling whiteness;
  The ear hearkened to the stillness of the solemn air;
No sound of wheel rumbling nor of foot falling,
And the busy morning cries came thin and spare.
  Then boys I heard, as they went to school, calling,
They gathered up the crystal manna to freeze
Their tongues with tasting, their hands with snow-balling;
  Or rioted in a drift, plunging up to the knees;
Or peering up from under the white-mossed wonder,
'O look at the trees!' they cried, 'O look at the trees!'
  With lessened load a few carts creak and blunder,
Following along the white deserted way,
A country company long dispersed asunder:
  When now already the sun, in pale display
Standing by Paul's high dome, spread forth below
His sparkling beams, and awoke the stir of the day.

For now doors open and war is waged with the snow;
And trains of sombre men, past tale of number,
Tread long brown paths as towards their toil they go:
But even for them no cares awhile encumber
Their minds diverted; the daily word unspoken,
The daily thoughts of labour and sorrow slumber
At the sight of the beauty that greets them, for the charm
they have broken.

Last in the 1884 book were these verses, deceptively simple for a later generation suspicious of headmasters and of calls to 'youth'. From the heart, outside our time, a paradox withdraws them from easy sentiment.

O youth whose hope is high,
Who dost to Truth aspire,
Whether thou live or die,
O look not back nor tire.

Thou that art bold to fly
Through tempest, flood and fire,
Nor dost not shrink to try
Thy heart in torments dire:

If thou canst Death defy,
If thy Faith is entire,
Press onward, for thine eye
Shall see thy heart's desire.

Beauty and love are nigh,
And with their deathless quire
Soon shall their eager cry
Be numbered and expire.

Twenty-four sonnets which Bridges called *The Growth of Love* had been published by Bumpus in 1876. Three years later his small and anonymous edition of twenty-two copies was printed by Daniel; and as Madan puts it, 'this greatly enlarged issue with seventy-nine sonnets can be fairly regarded as an *Editio Princeps*'. Madan's fair regard leaves me free to choose, but anyone wanting exact bibliographical reference may find it in the Appendix to Edward Thompson's book where six pages are given to 'Changes in the Text of *The Growth of Love*'. Though the October 1890 black-letter Daniel edition (one hundred copies) was 'a corrected reprint' I have chosen to use the 1889 private issue, as the first and because it remains the most attractive Daniel Press rarity. The numbering of these five sonnets is therefore from that version. They show Bridges in varied mood, praising, pausing, intimate and doubting – 'Disheartened pilgrims, I am one of you' – thriving upon the discipline of this form.

XVI

This world is unto God a work of art
Of which the unaccomplished heavenly plan
Lives in his masterpiece and grows with man
Unto perfection and success in part.
The ultimate creation stayed to start
From the last creature for whom all began:
Who child in what he is and what he can
Hath yet God's judgement and desire at heart.
  Knowledge denied him, and his little skill
Cumbered by laws he never can annul,
Baffled by qualities adverse and ill,
With feeble hands, few years and senses dull,
His art is nature's nature, and love still
Makes his abode with the most beautiful.

XXIV

O weary pilgrims chaunting of your woe
That turn your eyes to all the peaks that shine,
Hailing in each the citadel divine
The which ye thought to have entered along ago
Until at length your feeble steps and slow
Falter upon the threshold of the shrine,
And your hearts overburdened doubt in fine
Whether it be Jerusalem or no:
  Disheartened pilgrims, I am one of you,
For having worshipped many a barren face
I scarce now greet the goal I journeyed to:
I stand a pagan in the heavenly place,
Beneath the lamp of truth I am found untrue
And question with the glory I embrace.

XL

At times with hurried hoofs and scattering dust
I race by field or highway, and my horse
Spare not but urge direct in headlong course
Unto some fair far hill that gain I must:
But near arrived the vision soon mistrust,
Rein in and stand as one who sees the source
Of strong illusion, shaming thought to force
From off his mind the soil of passion's gust.
   My brow I bare then and with slackened speed
Can view the country pleasant on all sides
And to kind salutation give good heed.
I ride as one who for his pleasure rides
And stroke the neck of my delighted steed
And seek what cheer the village inn provides.

LIII

Come gentle sleep, I woo thee: come and take
Not now the child into thine arms, from fright
Composed by drowsy tune and shaded light,
Whom ignorant of thee thou didst nurse and make:
Nor now the boy who scorned thee for the sake
Of growing knowledge or mysterious night,
Tho' with fatigue thou didst his limbs invite
And heavily weigh the eyes he strove to wake:
   No, nor the man severe who from his best
Failing, alert fled to thee, that his breath,
Blood, force and fire should come at morn redrest:
But me, from whom thy comfort tarrieth,
For all my wakeful prayer sent without rest
To thee, O shew and shadow of my death.

LXXV

Ah heavenly joy! But who hath ever heard,
Who hath seen joy, or who shall ever find
Joy's language? There is neither speech nor word:
Nought but itself to teach it to mankind.
   Scarce in our twenty thousand painful days
We may touch something: but there lives – beyond
The best of art, or nature's kindest phase –
The hope whereof our spirit is fain and fond:

The cause of beauty given to man's desires,
Writ in the expectancy of starry skies,
The faith which gloweth in our fleeting fires,
The aim of all the excellence we prize:
Which but to love, pursue and pray for well
Maketh earth heaven, and to forget it, hell.

The five parts of Bridges' *Shorter Poems* were printed by Daniel in irregular order during 1893-4: 'January' and 'North Wind in October' are from Book v, which came second, because that group was making its first appearance. 'January' becomes more than merely descriptive in its final verse; 'North Wind' compares with 'London Snow' in experimental metre and precise phrasing. His last line offers redeeming optimism, if the poem is read as an allegory of mood.

JANUARY

Cold is the winter day, misty and dark:
The sunless sky with faded gleams is rent:
And patches of thin snow outlying, mark
The landscape with a drear disfigurement.

The trees their mournful branches lift aloft:
The oak with knotty twigs is full of trust,
With bud-thronged stems the cherry in the croft:
The chesnut holds her gluey knops upthrust.

No birds sing, but the starling chaps his bill
And chatters mockingly: the newborn lambs
Within their strawbuilt fold beneath the hill
Answer with plaintive cry their bleating dams.

Their voices melt in welcome dreams of spring,
Green grass and leafy trees and sunny skies:
My fancy decks the woods, the thrushes sing,
Meadows are gay, bees hum and scents arise.

And God the Maker doth my heart grow bold
To praise for wintry works not understood,
Who all the worlds and ages doth behold,
Evil and good as one, and all as good.

NORTH WIND IN OCTOBER

In the golden glade the chestnuts are fallen all:
From the sered boughs of the oak the acorns fall:
The beech scatters her ruddy fire,
The lime hath stripped to the cold
And standeth naked above her yellow attire:
The larch thinneth her spire
To lay the ways of the wood with cloth of gold.

Out of the golden-green and white
Of the brake the fir-trees stand upright
In the forest of flame, and wave aloft
To the blue of heaven their blue-green tuftings soft.

But swiftly in shuddering gloom the splendours fail,
As the harrying north-wind beareth
A cloud of skirmishing hail
The grieved woodland to smite:
In a hurricane through the trees he teareth
Raking the boughs and the leaves rending,
And whistleth to the descending
Blows of his icy flail.
Cold and snow he mixeth in spite
And whirleth afar, as away on his winnowing flight
He passeth, and all again for awhile is bright.

'Now in Wintry Delights', a neglected poem in the *Classical Prosody* group, has threefold fascination in Bridges' history, an attractive Daniel Press book, and as good fireside soliloquy to be read at a sitting. It was addressed to his old friend Lionel Muirhead. He was tempting providence with these long lines, indistinguishable except by pedants from his choice for *The Testament of Beauty*.

Now in wintry delights, and long fireside meditation,
'Twixt studies and routine paying due court to the Muses,
My solace in solitude, when broken roads barricade me
Mudbound, unvisited for months with my merry children,
Grateful t'ward Providence, and heeding a slander against me
Less than a rheum, think of me to-day, dear Lionel, and take
This letter as some account of Will Stone's versification.

History and SCIENCE our playthings are: what an untold
Wealth of inexhaustive treasure is stored up for amusement!
Shall the amass'd Earth-structure appeal to me less than in early
Childhood an old fives-ball, whose wraps I wondering unwound,
Untwining the ravel'd worsted, that mere rubbish and waste
Of leather and shavings had bound and moulded elastic
Into a perfect sphere? Shall not the celestial earth-ball
Equally entertain a mature enquiry, reward our
Examination of its contexture, conglomerated
Of layer'd debris, the erosion of infinite ages?
Tho' I lack the wizard Darwin's scientific insight
On the barren sea-beaches of East Patagonia gazing,
I must wond'ring attend, nay learn myself to decypher
Time's rich hieroglyph, with vast elemental pencil
Scor'd upon Earth's rocky crust, – minute shells slowly collecting
Press'd to a stone, uprais'd to a mountain, again to a fine sand
Worn, burying the remains of an alien organic epoch,
In the flat accretions of new sedimentary strata;
All to be crush'd, crumpled, confused, contorted, abandon'd,
Broke, as a child's puzzle is, to be recompos'd with attention;
Nature's history-book, which she hath torn as asham'd of;
And lest those pictures on her fragmentary pages
Should too lightly reveal frustrate Antiquity, hath laid
Ruin upon ruin, revolution upon revolution:
Yet no single atom, no least insignificant grain
But, having order alike of fate, and faulty disorder,
Holds a record of Time, very vestiges of Creation;
Which who will not attend scorns blindly the only commandments
By God's finger of old inscribed on table of earth-stone.

RICHARD WATSON DIXON

His friends and critics agree that in certain veins and passages Dixon found more success than in others – a critical point some distance short of profound, which applies to almost every poet who ever wrote except perhaps Bridges with his focus upon art and technique. 'Dixon's poetry cannot be defended against the charge of inequality', Bridges wrote, 'the occurrence of poor and faulty passages of various defect, which easily offend a taste that cannot relish his excellences . . .'. Hopkins remarked in a letter to Bridges (October 1881) that 'he is unequal and the unequality lies in execution, chiefly in his diction, which varies from rich to meagre'. Professor Abbott, introducing the volume of letters between Hopkins and Dixon, wrote: 'The admirable qualities of Dixon the man are insufficiently represented in his verses. It is as though he were writing with a veil between himself and life. Perhaps the word 'muffled' will do as well as any to mark this baffling quality'. Adding to the confusion, if one is to trouble with the game, Abbott thought Dixon 'more at ease when he has a suitable story to tell than when he is attempting lyric measures'; yet Hopkins, strictest of critics, could tell him (April 1881), 'I do not think it would be possible to find, for pure imagination, anything anywhere more beautiful than 'Fallen Rain'; and to Bridges (February 1887) expressed his opinion that 'The pathetic imagination of 'Sky that rollest ever' seems to me to have nothing like it but some of Coleridge in our literature'.

The several essays Bridges wrote on his poet friends form an attractive and private group, but it is hard to follow the sense of timing which seems ever to have been present in his mind. In 1911 he elected to edit the poems of Dolben whose death by drowning had occurred in 1867. Hopkins died in 1889 and Bridges produced him in 1918. An edition of Dixon's poems arrived earlier in 1909. There had been requests before, but 'I could not see in the public taste the sign of any feeling that would welcome the book, or even regard it with the respect necessary to its acceptance'.

In an innocent endearing way both had found Dixon awkward to meet at first. 'I fancied you were shy' wrote Hopkins (April

1882) with disarming openness after that one occasion when they came together as adults, after elaborate attempts had failed, 'and that time would have been needed for this to wear off'. Dixon responds with the detachment of one who has given up the social struggle: 'I dare say I seemed "shy": I have an unfortunate manner: & am constantly told that I am too quiet: I have often tried to overcome it: but the effort is always apparent to those with whom I am, & never succeeds'.

Bridges recalled in his essay the moment of their first meeting, on the platform of How Mill station near Dixon's parish in the north: 'His attitude and gait as he walked on the platform were those of a man who, through abstraction or indifference, is but half aware of his surroundings, and his attention to the train as he gazed along the carriages to discover me had that sort of awkwardness that comes from the body not expressing the intention of the mind'.

Was Bridges remembering Dixon's short poem 'The Mystery of the Body', with its puzzled question

> May I then a likeness find
> In the features of the mind
> And the antic of the flesh?

And did Dixon mirror the reflection of Macbeth?

> there's no art
> Can tell the mind's construction in the face.

Whatever critical ripples are discernible from the neglect of Dixon, he appears a lovable and suffering character without guile or enemies. Returning to him, to his poems for their own qualities rather than as reflections of criticism Hopkins offered, the solitude and independence of Dixon and his accurate diction in describing these may surprise us. The precision of melancholy in 'By the Sea' with its telling last phrase which shocks by turning the whole poem from description to metaphor; subtlety of his religious faith in the sonnet, 'Humanity'; fear for the disappearance of youthful inspiration in his ode 'The Spirit Wooed', or the heartfelt torment of a late poem, the 'Hymn' in which he prays for all-embracing forgiveness through penitence, with its final verse

And grant that I, when I forecast,
  And shrink in fear of coming things,
May take this comfort of the past,
  And lay it on my imaginings

– these and such others may represent now aspects of Dixon which Abbott half a century ago and others since have ignored. Dixon as the most private of poets accords with Bridges' portrait of him, with that lack of appreciation from any wider public that was recognised by Hopkins in the sensitive letter opening their correspondence, June 1878, '. . . I knew what I should feel myself in your position, if I had written and published works, the extreme beauty of which the author himself the most keenly feels, and they had fallen out of sight at once and been (you will not mind my saying it, as it is, I suppose, plainly true) almost wholly unknown . . .'

It also accords with his rescue or enrollment by Bridges as a Daniel Press poet. Brotherhoods were familiar to Dixon, as we have seen, at school and Oxford and after. At the close of the isolated years he seems to be entering another, not declared as such but conscious as a group. His *Odes and Eclogues* appeared in 1884: 'I now send you a pamphlet of poems' he wrote to Hopkins in April, 'which I have printed at Oxford, at Mr Daniel's press, where Bridges printed Prometheus. You do not like printing of this limited sort, I know: but apart from that, I shall be glad to know what you think. The London public have given up reading poetry. In fact this is not a literary age: & there seems to be a sort of feeling to retire on Oxford & strive to win the young'.

Dixon's melancholy was not spiritless. Bridges enjoyed his sense of humour, a mild pleasure in eccentricity, his shrewdness as historian and vigour at a sort of family tennis. His letters show more passionate distaste for certain aspects of Tennyson and Carlyle than could gain the assent of Hopkins in reply. Married twice, without children of his own, there is no hint that Dixon's domestic life was less than contented. Relative neglect of his qualities as priest and historian matched the silence which greeted his poetry. He has been called one of the last among amateur scholars, as author of a six volume *History of the Reformation*, for which in the last year of his life Dixon became Honorary Fellow of his old College at Oxford, and received an honorary degree as Doctor of Divinity. Recognition within the Church took him no further than minor Canon in the diocese of Carlisle, Rural Dean,

Examining Chaplain, all more burdensome than rewarding. Eccentricity is suggested by the casual note which ends a letter to Hopkins, October 1881: 'I ought to tell you that I am engaged to be married some time or other'.

The diffidence or in current phrase 'low profile' of a Victorian author makes its appeal now. Clough showed it in his verse and life, Kinglake in *Eothen*. When Kinglake approached the Holy Sepulchre in Jerusalem and felt no response we appreciate his courage in saying so. Dixon, poet of diffidence, dependably avoided excess, toed his line. Bernard Bergonzi in an excellent book about Hopkins calls Dixon 'an attractive but dim figure'. We could reckon him a poet of the dim, connoisseur of disappointment. It is an attractive vein, close to the more Christian term humility.

The rare quality of precision in humility lifts Dixon's poems to the level of his religious life: as a religious poet of the late nineteenth century we should read him again. James Sambrook, whose sympathetic biography* is the best source, admires his work 'when he tried to make serious verse not out of public themes but out of his own direct private experience, especially his experiences of loneliness, old age, melancholy and that very conflict of claims which arose from his impulse to retire back into the aesthetic dream world'.

But the aesthetic dream world was not what one would suppose in connection with the Morris circle of his youth. The 'Ode on Conflicting Claims', from that Daniel book which Hopkins received in 1884, is a successful poem expressing defiant right to ignore the state of the world,

> the many men,
> The unfed, the untaught,
> Who groan beneath that adamantine chain
> Whose tightness kills, whose slackness whips the flow
> Of waves of futile woe

and reach peacefully for some well-loved book,

> Reach some old volume down,
> Some poet's book, which in thy bygone years
> Thou hast consumed with joy as keen as fears,

**A Poet Hidden*. London, The Athlone Press, 1962.

When o'er it thou wouldst hang with rapturous frown,
Admiring with sweet envy all
The exquisite of words, the lance-like fall
Of mighty verses, each on each,
The sweetness which did never cloy,
(So wrought of thought ere touched with speech)
And ask again, Hast thou no right to joy.

It was a frequent theme with him, tacitly blaming the strict moralist as here, or complaining at the speed of nature's changes, or his own inability to absorb a scene as it deserved, wanting to experience transient beauty. Addressing himself in the same poem he defines his goal as

Beauty, the heart of beauty,
The sweetness, yea, the thoughtful sweetness,
The one right way in each, the best,
Which satisfies the soul,
The firmness lost in softness, the touch of typical meetness,
Which lets the soul have rest;
Those things to which thyself aspirest . . .

Bridges also aspired to beauty, an enfeebled word now but not then. This sort of 'aesthetic dream world' differed from that of *The Germ* thirty years earlier, in which Rossetti had recognised a Dreamland where 'most of the writers in that miraculous piece of literature seem to be'.

Dixon wrote his share of verse fiction, including the long poem *Mano* admired by Abbott and dutifully analysed by Sambrook who concludes it 'is comparable with the heroic achievement of the *Church History*'; but preferring privacy above heroism in poetry I shall choose among the quiet, often rather sad poems whose honesty reports the true borders of experience.

Some artistic justice relating to such poems produced in Dixon's lifetime a sort of balance between neglect and understanding. After miseries which were and are usual in schools, and his cheerful Oxford period where the inner circle called him Dickadees and others Black Dixon, only he and Fulford among the former followed their resolve to take Holy Orders. His eccentricities as curate of St Mary the Less, Lambeth, and of St Mary's, Newington Butts, the only metropolitan appointments in Dixon's church career, seem to have damaged his chances.

Marrying William Morris to Jane Burden, Dixon blundered by calling them 'William and Mary'. Bridges calls him 'a most unusual curate' and gives a story Dixon liked to tell, of 'that Lord's Day, when, having to offer thanks for the church warden who was sitting in his pew again for the first time after a dangerous illness, he proclaimed in a mighty voice that that gentleman desired to give praises to God for his safe deliverance from pain and peril of child-birth'.

His own marriage at the age of twenty-eight to a forty-year-old widow with three daughters, though unconventional seems to have been a happy one. In the same year his less fortunate step, joining the staff of Highgate School, produced over the years its marvellous result: Hopkins aged seventeen, a pupil there, knew him a little, but became well acquainted with his poetry from the copy of Dixon's first book, *Christ's Company*, given by the author to a Highgate master. That seed grew to the friendship which both needed, each separated by religious vocation from literary life.

He moved to Carlisle High School as Second Master after leaving Highgate through illness, though Highgate was something of a health resort in those days and such a change could equally have been reversed. At Carlisle we are not amazed to learn he could not keep order in the classroom; for, as his Headmaster gently expressed it, 'nature had not given him much of that indescribable power which makes boys feel that it is dangerous to go too far with a man'. In 1868 Dixon ended his career as teacher, accepting the less than brilliant invitation to become a minor canon and Honorary Librarian of Carlisle Cathedral. He was thirty-five.

Four years earlier the publication of *Christ's Company* had brought small attention from critics or public. The tale of neglect continues through a heroic period at his parish of Hayton in the diocese of Carlisle, to which he moved in 1875, where he laboured to complete volumes of his *History of the Reformation* and wrote *Mano*, a fictional epic of the tenth century, the manuscript of which remained unopened by his trusted clerical friend in the north who has my sympathetic understanding. To that period belong some of the shorter poems which would be printed by Daniel at Oxford.

So much for the worst of neglect, and misfortune: his first wife died in 1876. Alone in the north, with little encouragement for any among his endeavours as parish priest, poet or historian,

Dixon never lost touch with the circle of his Oxford friends. If we find it difficult to imagine him among that merry group which attempted frescoes in the Oxford Union, perhaps a shared melancholy prompted Rossetti in 1875 to write a generous long letter declaring 'that you are one of the most subtle as well as varied of our poets, and that the neglect of such work as yours on all hands is an incomprehensible accident'. Dixon replied, much moved: 'My work has met with nearly absolute neglect, but along with this there has been some censure of a very ignorant sort. Your approbation makes up for everything'.

And a new time of communion and encouragement started with the letter he received from Hopkins in June 1870. When Hall Caine was preparing an anthology of sonnets in 1880, these several loyal friends commended each other's work for inclusion: Rossetti wrote to Hall Caine, 'There is an admirable but totally unknown living poet named Dixon . . .'; the unknown poet persuaded Hopkins to submit sonnets, and there this chain reaction ceased, for by rejecting Hopkins the editor also lost Bridges.

It is disappointing that Dixon's second marriage so casually mentioned to Hopkins in a postscript, to Matilda Routledge the publisher's daughter, was not fruitful in the issue of children or literature. The firm published *Mano* and commissioned him to edit Routledge's *Bible Birthday Book*, but more might have been expected from such a father-in-law.

In his new and beautiful parish of Warkworth there is no doubt Dixon avoided temptations towards public life, withdrawing as candidate for the Chair of Poetry at Oxford. Occupied chronically with his *History* (which brought him to London sometimes), enjoying now the friendship of Hopkins as letter writer, with visits from Bridges whom Hopkins had introduced, and Mary Coleridge (sent by Bridges) who loved staying with friends in Northumberland, life assumed the sort of northern peace his temperament needed. The last wretched years of illness and breakdown produced some of his finest mystic poems, better recognised by Mary Coleridge than by Bridges.

For these late poems, Dixon received less than his due from Bridges, who in a more famous context gave only hesitant and measured commendation to Hopkins. These three friends, with Mary Coleridge of equal but less intimate importance, nursed their private convictions of creating a new poetry; they were the modern movement, possessing as to public appearance a patience which puzzles us now. It is the quality which held back the tide of

Bridges' achievement for its thundering effect in extreme old age, and had caused him to release the work of his old friends at long intervals of years, when the timing seemed right. James Sambrook has a perceptive comment on the moment when Hopkins introduced Dixon to Bridges, 'whose published verse, tiny in quantity and flawless in execution, was known in 1878 to few readers, and the three men formed a close circle of hidden poets, helping each other with encouragement and criticism. For Dixon his two new friends constituted a second Brotherhood'. In the privacy of Daniel's press it had a home.

Simon Nowell-Smith has described (*Times Literary Supplement*, December 13, 1957) how on two occasions Hopkins almost became a Daniel Press author. In 1880, at the start of his acquaintance with Daniel, Bridges proposed a composite volume, the work of five poets of whom four are identifiable as Dixon, Dolben, Hopkins and Bridges himself. Each would contribute four or five poems. Bridges allowed the idea to drop after Daniel had expressed misgivings about his competence as printer in accepting such responsibility; and the lack of evidence in any letter from Hopkins can be taken as proof that Bridges made his suggestion without consulting his authors, for Hopkins had told him a year earlier that 'publishing now is out of the question: when I say that I do not mean to publish I speak the truth'.

The saga of secrecy about Hopkins' work continued at his death, for within two months Patmore was writing to Bridges (in a letter quoted by Simon Nowell-Smith): 'I am very glad to know that you are to write a memorial of him. It is quite right that it should be privately printed. I, as one of his friends, should protest against any attempt to share him with the public, to whom little of what was most truly characteristic in him could be communicated'. Now this expresses a different scruple from any felt by Hopkins as to publication of his poems. After *The Wreck of the Deutschland* and *The Loss of the Eurydice* had in turn been rejected by *The Month*, 'he gave up trying to publish his poems, though he did not object to the idea of posthumous publication, if that were God's will'.* He worried as to the vanity of time spent writing verse, and would surely have shrunk from any notion of anxiety to get his work published, but he never suggested that contempt for 'the public' implied in Patmore's phrasing.

His own comments upon the Daniel Press in several letters

*Bernard Bergonzi, p. 85.

leave no doubt that Hopkins would not have wanted his poems printed privately there, in editions which unbelievably at that time looked expensive. In 1883 when Bridges' first Daniel book, *Prometheus the Firegiver*, appeared, Hopkins wrote to Dixon: 'This private printing of *Prometheus* may turn out unfortunate. I have myself no taste for what is called dainty in the get up of books and am altogether wanting in the spirit of a book hunter. 10s. seems like what is called a prohibitive price. I could not recommend our library to get such a book and till the second edition I shall not see the poem in print'.

To Bridges he had written a few weeks before: 'I cd. not venture to ask that our library should subscribe half a sovereign for an *édition de luxe* of a new book by an almost unknown author . . . I am rueful and remorseful about P.F. But what else could come of handmade Dutch paper? I regret that Daniel made his offer.'

Next year Dixon sent him the Daniel printing of his own *Odes and Eclogues*, with half an apology: 'I now send you a pamphlet of poems which I have printed at Oxford, at Mr Daniel's press, where Bridges printed *Prometheus*. You do not like printing of this sort, I know; but apart from that, I shall be glad to know what you think'. Hopkins within a few days wrote something of what he thought in a letter to Bridges: 'Canon Dixon sends me from Warkworth a little volume of Daniel's printing. I like the get-up better than *Prometheus*. It seems there is even some advantage in publishing in this way; at least he says so, but it would be tedious to explain how, AND WHAT DOES ANYTHING AT ALL MATTER?'. Many historians of books floundering to define a private press would happily settle for that last sentence and sentiment.

It would be wrong to suppose the mutual criticism in exchanges between Hopkins, Dixon and Bridges provided that admiration which public neglect withheld. One great merit of Hopkins was to offer fearless comment in flawless prose. When the time came for an opinion about *The Feast of Bacchus*, the other play Daniel printed for Bridges, no warmer commendation was at first available than 'In its kind, then, which has for me no attraction, and in its metre, which has to me no beauty, I think it a masterpiece'. Hopkins sometimes makes one think of Oscar Wilde, both classicists, in the disciplined precision of his prose. 'I do not think it desirable that I shd. be wholly uninfluenced by you or you by me' he wrote to Bridges in April 1897; 'one ought to be independant but not unimpressionable: that wd. be to refuse education'. Over the use of sprung rhythm a mild rivalry sprang between them, important as a worry to Bridges in offering Hopkins' poems for publication before his own practice in this theme had gained recognition. A little of the passion, controlled in gentlemanly fashion, beneath the Boar's Hill withdrawal appears if we trace that theme.

Between Hopkins and Dixon, closer in piety further apart in age, friction was unthinkable. Their roles had partly changed, the young Highgate master become middle-aged friend and pupil. Hopkins found less to admire in later packages of manuscript which reached him from Warkworth; one wishes he had seen those last religious poems, which Bridges could not thoroughly accept.

Hopkins, an effeminate aesthete perhaps, mentally enclosed with the Jesuits, sensitive in portraits, was ever a robust and fearless correspondent, sharpening the knife of language as critic or reporter. Here are two instances from a time when Bridges was ill: 'The great gale, which you must have felt at Torquay, was here terrible, nearly killed two of us, left a scene of havoc, and knocked all round our neighbourhood tall trees down like ninepins'. Of cuckoos: 'When they perch they sing wrong at first, I mean they correct their first try, raising the upper note. The interval varies as much as from less than a minor third to nearly as much as a common fourth and this last is the time when the bird is in loud and good song'.

His admiration will be evidence of our folly in forgetting Dixon, though Hopkins generally considered the poems 'unequal', and if sifted his praise applies only in part to poetic success, part to holiness of character. As it would be improper to quote what I find acceptable and ignore the rest, here is a long passage from his letter to Bridges, 22 October 1881:

> I suppose that I have all Canon Dixon's MS pieces by me that you have seen excepting the two epic works. The best of all, I am inclined to think, is the *Ode on Conflicting Claims,* at least the execution is nearly perfect and on a level with the thought and feeling, in which he is always a master and never makes a false note. This poem is one of extreme excellence. But he is unequal and the unequality lies in execution, chiefly in his diction, which varies from rich to meagre. He has not a sure hand like Tennyson and will let fall a weak stanza: this is

against his success. His command of pathos is exquisite and he excels in all tragic feeling, and that with an extreme purity, a directness of human nature, and absence of affectation which is most rare. I feel in reading him what a gentleman he is and it brings on that feeling that I am a blackguard. His other great excellence is pure imagination, either arising from images in nature (as in the Rainbow poem) or expressing itself in them: I think it would not be possible in literature to find a lovelier example than that Rainbow piece. I hope he will push on with the epic or romance you saw, for he will be more telling in a long than in short pieces, as is natural in one who is rich in matter and imperfect in form. I see no reason why he should not write the finest narrative poem of this age: he will never acquire Tennyson's workmanship and infallibly telling freedom of stroke, which is indeed half of art, but he much excels him in other gifts.

To Dixon he could be profoundly complimentary, though Hopkins as critic seldom offered mere admiration. As their correspondence opened, he wrote in a general summary, September 1878: 'As far as I am concerned I say with conviction and put it on record again that you have great reason to thank God who has given you so astonishingly clear an inward eye to see what is in visible nature and in the heart such a deep insight into what is earnest, tender, and pathetic in human life and feeling as your poems display'. In April 1881 from Liverpool he tells Dixon: 'I do not think it would be possible to find, for pure imagination, anything anywhere more beautiful than *Fallen Rain*'.

He was trying to set to music 'Sky that rollest ever', and later in the same letter declares it 'will always be in my mind when I see blue and white in running streams ravelled and unravelled by the current'. In October of the same year he gives a general view again: 'A True humanity of spirit, neither mawkish on the one hand nor blustering on the other, is the most precious of all qualities in style, and this I prize in your poems, as I do in Bridges'.

Such moral judgements are remote from modern opinion as expressed in Sambrook's biography, that 'in the shorter poems nearly all his best work is in a thin imaginative vein where he uses certain autumnal scenes to express a personal awareness of mortality'. Though I shall leave aside the longer poems, a higher claim than this will be made for Dixon as poet.

Hopkins had a curious exchange with Bridges on the qualities of a gentleman, and wrote in February 1883 'that gentlemen do not pander to lust or other basenesses nor, as you say, give themselves airs and affectations nor do other things to be found in modern works. And this adds a charm to everything Canon Dixon writes, that you feel he is a gentleman and thinks like one'. But if we recall the 'unequal' character of Dixon's work, as he and Bridges and other have agreed, it should be balanced by Hopkins on Blake in his letter to Dixon, December 1887: 'I have Blake's poems by me. Some of them much remind me of yours. The best are of an exquisite freshness and lyrical inspiration, but there is mingled with the good work a great deal of rubbish, want of sense, and some touches of ribaldry and wickedness'.

Such sentences might now tempt a reader to dismiss Hopkins as critic, which would be absurd. The point for our limitless uncritical admiration of Blake is not that Hopkins thought him morally unreliable, but that he found 'mingled with the good work a great deal of rubbish'.

It was when Dixon's second Daniel Press volume, *Lyrical Poems*, reached him that Hopkins wrote to Bridges, February 1887, 'there is in him a view of truly matchless beauty: it is not always the whole texture but a thread in it and sometimes the whole web is of that . . . The pathetic imagination of *Sky that rollest ever* seems to me to have nothing like it but some of Coleridge in our literature'.

Dixon's first Daniel book, *Odes and Eclogues*, appeared in 1884. Leaving aside the narrative poems, of which the Daniel Press *Story of Eudocia and her Brothers* is a longish instance, it is difficult to isolate among the simple songs and descriptive melancholy, representing him in a few examples, Dixon's voice. 'Ode on Conflicting Claims' shows a scholar-parson troubled by social conscience; 'To a Bramble in Winter', closely observed, may be read as allegory of his own depression as age reduced his artistic responses. Both are from *Odes and Eclogues*.

ODE ON CONFLICTING CLAIMS

Hast thou no right to joy,
Oh youth grown old, who palest with the thought
Of the measureless annoy,
The pain and havoc wrought
By Fate on man: and of the many men,

The unfed, the untaught,
Who groan beneath that adamantine chain
Whose tightness kills, whose slackness whips the flow
Of waves of futile woe:
Hast thou no right to joy?

Thou thinkest in thy mind
In thee it were unkind
To revel in the liquid Hyblian store,
While more and more the horror and the shame,
The pity and the woe grow more and more,
Persistent still to claim
The filling of thy mind.

Thou thinkest that if none in all the rout
Who compass thee about
Turn full their soul to that which thou desirest,
Nor seek to gain thy goal,
Beauty, the heart of beauty,
The sweetness, yea, the thoughtful sweetness,
The one right way in each, the best,
Which satisfies the soul,
The firmness lost in softness, the touch of typical meetness,
Which lets the soul have rest;
Those things to which thyself aspirest:–
That they, though born to quaff the bowl divine,
As thou art, yield to the strict law of duty;
And thou from them must thine example take,
Leave the amaranthine vine,
And the prized joy forsake.

Oh thou, foregone in this,
Long struggling with a world that is amiss,
Reach some old volume down,
Some poet's book, which in thy bygone years
Thou hast consumed with joys as keen as fears,
When o'er it thou wouldst hang with rapturous frown,
Admiring with sweet envy all
The exquisite of words, the lance-like fall
Of mighty verses, each on each,
The sweetness which did never cloy,
(So wrought of thought ere touched with speech),

And ask again, Hast thou no right to joy.
Take the most precious tones that thunder-struck thine ears
In gentler days gone by:
And if they yield no more the old ecstasy,
Then give thyself to tears.

TO A BRAMBLE IN WINTER

Oh thou that sinkest lower, changing now
Into a vermeil russet thy green brow,
Is then the youth, that once shone clear and bright,
Within thee still? Need I but think aright,
And in thy weak leaves, bibulous of rain,
And flaccid stem, I shall behold again
The trim, thorn-guarded vigour of thy prime,
And the green boldness of thy summer time,
Which dashed Jove's shower from thine unaltered face,
And still maintained thy reappearing grace,
When the winds shook, but could not rifle thee?
  Oh, still would I believe thee blithe and free,
See thy flowers still, and then thy cherished germ
Nodding to ripeness all the summer's term,
And richly deepening: still would I confess
In later months thy freshness not the less
When all were trembling, when the beech turned brown,
And life's last relics sought the foxglove's crown,
As sunk the year. But now, alas, behold
How droop thy fans! Some secret touch of cold
Trails thy rings lower, and relaxes all
The brave-spread stiffness of thy banners tall.
The bird that on thy shaken coil may light
Trusts not his little weight to thy weak might,
But beats his wings till he may spring from thee.
Playfellow of the winds no more, thy glee
Invites them not: the dark heaven-wandering rain
Or smites or spares thee with the like disdain.

Eudocia had never caused high expectations. 'Instead of fifteen copies of the Story of Eudocia & her Brothers', Dixon wrote to the printer in August 1887, 'I should be glad if you will kindly strike off twenty five: of which I will take fifteen'. And a month later, 'I think now that we had better have fifty copies printed, instead of twenty five'. As to the author, perhaps his optimism never rose higher than in estimating that 'a bit of plain unpretending narrative might do the English Muse good',* though the benefit could only have been of a restricted sort. Dixon thought the heroic couplet 'the most difficult thing in English versification'. *Eudocia* remains in the vein of metrical experiment.

From *Lyrical Poems*, printed by Daniel in 1887, I choose one of Dixon's successful and curiously questioning poems, with a heavy title 'The Mystery of the Body'; and a complex thought housed in simple form, 'Man's Coming'; and the 'Song' Hopkins praised.

THE MYSTERY OF THE BODY

Smiling with a pliant grace
   Rose on me a learned face:
Smiled the soul when smiled the eyes? –
   Up when ran the traceries
Of the forehead arching high,
Did the inner faculty
Tempering the hidden nerve
Mould the momentary curve,
Waking motions strange between
Spirit fine and fleshly screen?
   May I then a likeness find
In the features of the mind
And the antic of the flesh?
Wherefore should the wrinkled mesh
Of the forehead arching high
Image the soul's pleasantry?

MAN'S COMING

The world was gay and blithe:
   Again the world was sad:
Time moved his ceaseless scythe,
   Time, neither sad nor glad.

*This and the two sentences quoted above are from letters at Worcester College.

Then dragon dragon tore;
  Then swept their sheeted breath:
A spasm was at the core,
  From the rent flesh rose Death.

No more than this there was –
  Pain, rage, and Death through pain:
No more than this had cause
  To be in land or main.

'Twas thus before man came:
  He came, and with him guilt:
He bent a brow of shame
  On blood that had been spilt.

He cast an eye of care
  On pain, on rage through pain:
And these were made aware
  How awful was their reign.

And Death, that was at most
  Carcase and skeleton,
Became a shadowy host
  After the flesh and bone.

SONG

Sky, that rollest ever,
  It is given to thee
To roll above the river
  Rolling to the sea.

Truer is thy mirror
  In the lake or sea;
But thou lovest error
  More than constancy.

And the river running
  Fast into the sea,
His wild hurry shunning
  All thy love and thee;

Not a moment staying
To return thy smiles,
Sees thee still displaying
All thy sunny wiles:

Till thou fallest weeping:
Then more furiously
All his wild waves leaping
Rush into the sea.

'By the Sea' is included as fair instance of Dixon's melancholy; the sonnet 'Humanity', disciplined expression of a complex thought, shows that Jung was not the first to imagine a Collective Unconscious; and 'The feathers of the willow', so much admired by Hopkins, may be understood as the poet's solitude or depression as middle age approached. All three are from *Historic Odes and Other Poems*, published by Smith, Elder in 1864. In leaving Dixon one should read his moving and sad 'Hymn' which was published posthumously in the volume introduced by Mary Coleridge.

BY THE SEA

In tottering rain, like shadows, silently
The old pier-timbers struggle from the sea;
Strained in old storms by those wild waves that creep
So gently now, no longer do they keep
The pier that on them rested long ago,
But stand as driven piles in tottering row.
The sky sails downward, upward creeps the wave,
For countless clouds toward the sun's bright grave
Move curiously with grey and misty wing;
So thickly all the sky environing,
That only by one pale bright spot is known
Where still the sunken light is upward thrown,
And lately sunk the weary king of day:
Still on the sands below in stealthy play
Arise the billows of the nightly tide;
Each with its own clear layer doth override
The spreaded calm where its last brother rolled;
Each upon other rippling draws the fold
Of its thin edge along the soakëd sand,

And stirs the spongy foam 'twixt sea and land,
And lifts the dark waifs higher on the shore.
Yet in this quietness resides the roar
Of ocean floods; one rising of that wind,
And those slow clouds would leave the night behind
In bitter clearness; those cold waves would roll
In snarling billows white. So of the soul.

HUMANITY: A SONNET

There is a soul above the soul of each,
  A mightier soul, which yet to each belongs:
There is a sound made of all human speech,
  And numerous as the concourse of all songs:
And in that soul lives each, in each that soul,
  Though all the ages are its lifetime vast;
Each soul that dies, in its most sacred whole
  Receiveth life that shall for ever last.
And thus for ever with a wider span
  Humanity o'erarches time and death;
Man can elect the universal man,
  And live in life that ends not with his breath,
And gather glory that increaseth still
Till Time his glass with Death's last dust shall fill.

SONG

The feathers of the willow
Are half of them grown yellow
  Above the swelling stream;
And ragged are the bushes
And rusty now the rushes,
  And wild the clouded gleam.

The thistle now is older,
His stalk begins to moulder,
  His head is white as snow;
The branches all are barer,
The linnet's song is rarer,
  The robin pipeth now.

HYMN

O Lord my God, when sore bested
   My evil life I do bewail,
What times the life I might have led
   Arising smites me like a flail:

When I regard the past of sin,
   Till sorrow drown me like despair;
The saint in me that might have been
   With that I am when I compare:

Then grant the life that might have been
   To be in fact through penitence;
All my past years discharged of sin,
   And spent in grace and innocence:

And grant that I, when I forecast,
   And shrink in fear of coming things,
May take this comfort of the past,
   And lay it on my imaginings.

Amen.

MARY COLERIDGE

Mary Elizabeth Coleridge, great-niece of Samuel Taylor Coleridge, born in 1861 and dying at the early age of forty-six, shared in the brotherhood of the Daniel Press as Christina Rossetti had in the pre-Raphaelite Brotherhood. Bridges happened upon her poems after meeting her in 1895, and Daniel printed them the next year. This was her first appearance in print as a poet, though a novel *The Seven Sleepers of Ephesus* had been published in 1893. The *Dictionary of National Biography* entry makes a surprising error in saying that her poems came from Oxford University Press.

As she had friends in Northumberland – excellent friendships which took her often to Chillingham and to Bamborough Castle – Bridges introduced her to Dixon whom she loved to visit. Her essay, 'The Hermit of Warkworth' gives an account of him. In her turn Mary Coleridge introduced to the Daniel Press another poet, Ethel Wedgwood, whose book *Wind Along the Waste* appeared there anonymously in 1902.

This characteristic anonymity, affected first by Bridges, afflicted Mary Coleridge also. Her collection of poems, *Fancy's Following*, was 'by Anodos', a curious pseudonym, 'taken from George Macdonald's romance, *Phantastes*', as we learn from Madan, 'where it is evidently intended to bear the meaning of "wanderer"'. 'May I ask you, please,' she had written to the printer,* 'not to mention my name to anyone? I do not want it to appear. I had chosen Vespertilio as a nom de plume, but last summer a book of poems called Vespertilia something or other was published; so perhaps it had better be Nukteris, which has the same meaning? or Anodos'. Anonymity was one aspect of Daniel's press, shelter from the vulgar world. Even the black-letter of Bridges' *Shorter Poems*, giving, in Madan's well-known phrase, 'just the check to hasty reading which thoughtful and elaborate poems need', was of that kind, though less so than the first *Growth of Love* in an edition of twenty-two copies and unsigned. As the second *Growth of Love*, 1890, was printed by

*Correspondence in Worcester College.

Daniel in black-letter, the fortunate collector may choose between unsigned rarity and a check to hasty reading.

In the eighteen nineties it was not necessary for women to publish anonymously, but both Mary Coleridge and her friend Mrs Wedgwood were allowing very private poems to appear. The pretence of a secret is understandable.

Introducing a posthumous volume of her prose* Edith Sichel, who had also been responsible for the *Dictionary of National Biography* notice, wrote a sympathetic memoir of Mary Coleridge. She must have been a strange and brilliant person, independent, private, one of several young ladies devoting themselves in Hampstead to the study of Greek and to William Johnson Cory who taught them. At the age of thirteen she had met him, and ever afterwards according to Edith Sichel 'she loved cyclamen and irises, because they were favourites of his'. As an author she was unusual in disliking conversational reference to her books, 'and could hardly answer questions about them'. Her waywardness comes to us in two more sentences from Edith Sichel's memoir: 'At all times of her life she had an unaccountable faculty for finding the dull and dowdy delightful'; and 'it was dangerous to bring her within earshot of an egoist, for egoists always captivated her'.

Two facets of her poetry may captivate us, of which one was a privacy of intellect, an originality. Here is a simple brief poem, from the volume of *Collected Poems:*

Where, to me, is the loss
  Of the scenes they saw – of the sounds they heard;
A butterfly flits across,
  Or a bird;
The moss is growing on the wall,
  I heard the leaf of the poppy fall.

Her oddity and modernity are in its title, *No Newspapers.*

Something of her character, easily understandable to our age which becomes sensitive to the theme, is in an untitled poem from the same volume:

**Gathered Leaves from the Prose of Mary E. Coleridge*, London, Constable, 1910.

The fire, the lamp, and I, were alone together.
Out in the street it was wild and windy weather.

The fire said, 'Once I lived, and now I shine.
I was a wood once, and the wind was mine'.

The lamp said, 'Once I lived and was the Sun.
The fire and I, in those old days, were one'.

The fire said, 'Once I lived and saw the Spring.
I die in smoke to warm this mortal thing.'

The lamp said, 'I was once alive and free.
In smoke I die to let this mortal see.'

Then I remembered all the beasts that died
That I might eat and might be satisfied.

Then I remembered how my feet were shod,
Thought of the myriad lives on which I trod,

And sighed to feel that as I went my way,
I was a murderer ninety times a day.

One other from that collection should be quoted as showing her independence of thought, far from conventional charity of that time but recalling a tormented part of Mary Coleridge, her care for the poor. She taught them, at home and in the Working Women's College, but no such relationship as hers with Cory could reappear. Victorian spinsters of independent means spent time with the poor, by social contract, but 'it was a profound disappointment', Edith Sichel writes, 'when at last it dawned upon her that her hope could not be realised – that the obstacle to true equality lay, not only in the rich, but in the poor themselves'. This dawning is expressed with total honesty in her poem called 'An Insincere Wish Addressed to a Beggar':

We are not near enough to love,
  I can but pity all your woe;
For wealth has lifted me above,
  And falsehood set you down below.

If you were true, we still might be
  Brothers in something more than name;
And were I poor, your love to me
  Would make our differing bonds the same.

But golden gates between us stretch,
  Truth opens her forbidding eyes;
You can't forget that I am rich
  Nor I that you are telling lies.

Love never comes but at love's call,
  And pity asks for him in vain;
Because I cannot give you all,
  You give me nothing back again.

And you are right with all your wrong,
  For less than all is nothing too;
May Heaven beggar me ere long,
  And Truth reveal herself to you!

Of the several essays on his friends and their work, none was more heartfelt or perceptive than an essay on 'The Poems of Mary Coleridge' which Bridges wrote for *The Cornhill* a couple of months after her death in 1907. It would be best to reproduce it here, but I have no right to do so, and anyone may make his own journey through her work. After praising her gaiety and unexpected wit, Bridges seems to isolate two qualities of her poetry, a mysticism which Mary Coleridge herself reckoned a sort of defensible nonsense ('Meaning is to poetry what morals are to life', she wrote with shattering conciseness) and in certain short poems a brilliant expression of her solitude. This latter quality brought her with especial aptness into the Daniel Press.

She wrote with a discreet grief, so that reading just those few poems which make up *Fancy's Following* one imagines the nearly impossible self-control which governed her life. As a self-portrait this marvellous collection shows us heartbreak governed by the perfect manners of her intelligence. Sentiment is ruled out, unacceptable. Bridges quotes several, but here is another:

'HE KNOWETH NOT THAT THE DEAD ARE THINE'*

The weapon that you fought with was a word,
And with that word you stabbed me to the heart.
Not once but twice you did it, for the sword
  Made no blood start.

They have not tried you for your life. You go
Strong in such innocence as men will boast.
They have not buried me. They do not know
  Life from its ghost.

Several times in her perfectly disciplined stanzas violent metaphor shocks, as in these two called 'Mortal Combat':†

It is because you were my friend,
I fought you as the Devil fights.
Whatever fortune God may send,
For once I set the world to rights.

And that was when I thrust you down,
And stabbed you twice and twice again,
Because you dared take off your crown,
And be a man like other men.

In suggesting a close comparison with Dixon's poems, Bridges leaves out of account this vein of violence held down by the iron bands of breeding and formal brevity. Simplest in this kind is her single verse,

I have forgèd me in sevenfold heats
  A shield from foes and lovers,
And no one knows the heart that beats
  Beneath the shield that covers.

Housman would seem sometimes a closer companion for such poetry than Dixon whose puzzled melancholy and disappointment gave no hint of this bitter repression. The simplicity can rest half-understood, as in the verse called 'Confidence':

*From *Fancy's Following*, p. 39. †From *Fancy's Following*, p. 30.

Even to one I dare not tell
Where lies my Heaven, where lies my Hell;
But to the world will I confide
What's hid from all the world beside.

It seems to explain the fact of printed revelation, even in this small edition of one hundred and twenty-five copies and sheltered by a pseudonym. Bridges persuaded her. 'These verses owe much to one whose name the writer honours too highly to set it here', we read in smallest capitals opposite the opening poem.

It would have been hard for Bridges to write a more affectionate tribute than in the final paragraph of his essay, where he judges that the poems of Mary Coleridge, rather than her prose which he greatly admires, will be her finest monument.

> And it is the intimacy and spontaneity of her poems that will give them their chief value. They will be her portrait, an absolutely truthful picture of a wondrously beautiful and gifted spirit, whom thought could not make melancholy, nor sorrow sad: not in conventional attitude, nor with fixed features, nor lightly to be interpreted, nor even always to be understood, but mystical rather and enigmatical; a poetic effigy, the only likeness of worth; a music self-born of her contact with the wisdom and passion of the world, and which all the folly and misery of man could provoke only to gentle and loving strains.

Here are three more poems from her only Daniel Press book, *Fancy's Following*, 1896.

A MOMENT

The clouds had made a crimson crown
Above the mountains high.
The stormy sun was going down
In a stormy sky.

Why did you let your eyes so rest on me,
And hold your breath between?
In all the ages this can never be
As if it had not been.

'HE CAME UNTO HIS OWN AND HIS OWN RECEIVED HIM NOT.'

As Christ the Lord was passing by,
He came, one night, to a cottage door.
He came, a poor man, to the poor;
He had no bed whereon to lie.

He asked in vain for a crust of bread,
Standing there in the frozen blast.
The door was locked and bolted fast.
'Only a beggar!' the poor man said.

Christ the Lord went further on,
Until He came to a palace gate.
There a king was keeping his state,
In every window the candles shone.

The king beheld Him out in the cold.
He left his guests in the banquet hall.
He made his servants tend them all.
'I wait on a Guest I know of old.'

' 'Tis only a beggar-man!' they said.
'Yes,' he said, 'it is Christ the Lord.'
He spake to Him a kindly word,
He gave Him wine and he gave Him bread.

Now Christ is Lord of Heaven and Hell,
And all the words of Christ are true.
He touched the cottage and it grew;
He touched the palace and it fell.

The poor man is become a king.
Never was man so sad as he.
Sorrow and Sin on the throne make three,
He has no joy in mortal thing.

But the sun streams in at the cottage door
That stands where once the palace stood,
And the workman, toiling to earn his food,
Was never a king before.

WINGED WORDS

As darting swallows skim across a pool,
Whose tranquil depths reflect a tranquil sky,
So, o'er the depths of silence, dark and cool,
  Our wingèd words dart playfully,
    And seldom break
    The quiet surface of the lake,
      As they flit by.

ETHEL KATE WEDGWOOD

Ethel Kate Wedgwood's poems came to Daniel at the suggestion of Mary Coleridge, so extending the small circle of friends and in particular of women poets printed at the Daniel Press. Madan calls her poems 'lively and various in style'. In the good old-fashioned way he makes no mention of poignant tragedy, for the 1902 volume* begins with four stanzas of anonymous dedication in large italic to her husband, ending:

How should I use another name
Than that our household loves to hear?
– Nor yet could hawk for vulgar fame
What we have shared for many a year.

And so the space a blank shall go –
– You know the word its silence hides, –
To whom already, long ago,
Was dedicated all besides.

Josiah Wedgwood, politician, soldier, member of the brilliant group of men in the settlement of South Africa after the Boer War remembered as the Milner Kindergarten, had divorced his wife in a wretched and notorious case a couple of years before Madan wrote. Ethel Kate, the poet, had left him in 1913.

Lively and various was a vague phrase to use of her poems. One among them, 'In the Land of Lost Reputations', is much in the mood of Mary Coleridge:

Raise no stone above his head
 To mock at the unhonoured dead:–
 Ambition, failure, deep disgrace
 Lie hushed within this hiding-place:–

**Wind Along the Waste.*

Wherein he erred, let critics say,
– It was the gossip of the day, –
Time and Place gazettes record, –
  But the Angel of the Lord
  Perceiving how he strove and fell,
  Entered simply – 'He fought well'.

That as a poem of forgiveness, and the verse which finishes her book between a double arrangement of printer's flowers, deserve to be remembered:

I looked on the earth:– it was wintry and old:–
I looked in my heart:– it was wearied and cold:–
I looked in the eyes of the child I bare, –
And the soul of the world lived laughing there.

Her opening sonnet is also worth recall. I write on the last day of this year, season of parties, loud talk, hard hearing and filled glasses. Her poem of withdrawal strikes with especial sympathy:

Forests and waving pine-tree-tops, that sigh
Soft to yourselves beneath a clear, dark sky –
Although there be not so much breeze as thrills
The slenderest chord of any wind-stirred lyre;
Oracular streams that, flowing, never tire
Of lisping broken secrets to the hills
Under a mystic moon, – into your night
Receive us! Fevered, from the noisy light
Of yonder chambers truant-like we fly
Back into midnight's cool serenity,
Back to the winking stars of misty blue:

  Upon our forehead sinks the heavenly wind,
  The Purifier, and, with a falling dew,
  The holy silence of the better mind.

ALICE BUCKTON

From a note in the Worcester College correspondence:

> Miss E. Martineau thanks Revd. C. H. Daniel for two copies duly received of Miss A. Buckton's Poems, & now sends enclosed cheque for 15/0 in payment, as per account therewith. She would be glad to learn whether a cheaper & more convenient edition is likely to appear, & *how soon*. The old-fashioned type, rough uncut [pages] &c of this 'edition de luxe' strike her as *drawbacks*, rather than inducement to pay the high price at which this select & small edition has been issued.

Though there is no good reason to make them so, women poets almost create a separate theme within the Daniel Press: Margaret Woods, Mary Coleridge, Julia Wedgwood, Michael Field, Alice Buckton. Independent of literary fashion as the printer was of typographic fashion, they arrived by the privacy of friendship and introduction. Alice Buckton, Madan tells us, wrote a book called *Eager Heart*, a phrase which conveys the mood of her poems in the volume which must stand as least successful among Bridges' introductions to Daniel, *Through Human Eyes*. If we live beyond range of her intensity that may be because W. S. Gilbert had already satirized it in *Patience*, but nobody should undervalue what Bridges admired. Madan describes the poems as 'on religious and emotional subjects'. He also suggests that the opening poem, by Bridges himself, was written 'in the person of the poetess, describing *her* feelings', because when Elkin Mathews brought out a trade edition that poem had above it a phrase, 'The Singer speaks'.* This charming poem, less simple that at first sight, like so much in Bridges, makes a disappointing collection memorable. As for Alice Buckton, whose later and larger volume also seems commonplace, one poem called *Mountain Saxifrage* is worth recall. It has a sub-title, 'On the Stelvio Pass':

*The point is confirmed by correspondence at Worcester College.

By what divinest touch of Alchemy
Did barren rock and thin blue air combine
To build a thing so delicately fine,
Native with joy, and perfect power to be?
What force could draw the senseless atoms high,
And, out of dew, and cloud, and common clay,
Compose this magically fair array –
These breathing children of the earth and sky,
Were it not e'en the same resistless grace
That weaveth fiercest elements in place;
And, mixing vaster music out of strife,
Draweth from hells below, and heavens above
The slumbering mystery the world calls Life,
The waking Life th' adoring soul calls Love!

For much of the rest her mood was near to Dixon's, lacking in its expression his discretion or taste.

MARGARET L. WOODS

Though Margaret L. Woods came into Daniel's press by the simplest route, old friendship with the printer, there were other connections too. We have seen how she and her husband, President of Trinity, invited the young Laurence Binyon to dine with Bridges at their cottage on Boar's Hill on a summer evening in 1890.

Margaret Woods had a poem in *The Garland of Rachel.* Vacuous and inconsequential as her poem now seems, Symonds praised it and admired her among several 'unprofessional poets' who contributed to *The Garland.* She turned professional, with *Lyrics and Ballads* coming from a trade publisher in 1889 and a stout volume of *Collected Poems* in 1914. The preface to her verse play *The Princess of Hanover*, published by Duckworth in 1902, shows her as well acquainted with Bridges' views about stress and prosody, argues for oral rather than merely visual rhymes, and ends: 'Those who have accepted the principle of stressed verse may find much to criticise in mine, but not much that requires explanation.'

When C. M. Falconer wanted letters from all the *Garland* poets for his private manuscript copy of the book, the best that could be managed from her was a signature. 'Mrs Woods I got upon her return to Oxford', Daniel explained helpfully in a letter. (One might note here – it is unlikely to be noted elsewhere – that those stanzas with the title 'Little Gilbert Speaks', which came with doubtful sense into *The Garland*, were reprinted in *Collected Poems* as 'Little Gilbert to Little Rachel During her Illness'. He of course was little Gilbert Woods. Not a stunning literary revelation, but students of *The Garland* could wonder as to Gilbert's identity, and why he opened his mouth at all.)

Charmingly printed, especially in the second collection called *Songs*, 1896, two poems of differing mood seem now worth recalling, both from the volume of *Lyrics*, 1888. 'Passing' is a love poem without elaborate overtones:

With thoughts too lovely to be true,
With thousand, thousand dreams I strew
The path that you must come. And you
  Will find but dew.

I set an image in the grass,
A shape to smile on you. Alas!
It is a shadow in a glass –
  And so will pass.

I break my heart here, love, to dower
With all its inmost sweet your bower.
What scent will greet you in an hour?
  The gorse in flower.

Perhaps the sting, or thorn, is in the last line. And the opening poem, called 'Rest', attracts still in the Daniel book as an evocation of Oxford a century ago:

  To spend the long warm days
Silent upon the silent-stealing streams,
  To see, not gaze,
To hear, not listen, thoughts exchanged for dreams:

  See clouds that slowly pass
Trailing their shadows o'er the far faint down,
  And ripening grass,
While yet the meadows wear their starry crown:

  To hear the breezes sigh
Cool in the silver leaves like falling rain,
  Pause and go by,
Tired wanderers o'er the solitary plain:

  See far from all affright
Shy river creatures play hour after hour,
  And night by night
Low in the West the white moon's folding flower.

  Thus lost to human things,
To blend at last with Nature and to hear
  What song she sings
Low to herself when there is no one near.

Or perhaps she was remembering a day with the Daniels on the Thames in their house-boat. 'I can see it now' she wrote in her *Memoir* of Daniel*, 'journeying reluctantly back to Oxford at the end of a crowded summer, down the quiet silver reaches of the river below Buscot'. And so that we do not think of Margaret Woods as a too earnest spirit, it is well to end with her vignette of a chaotic morning in that boat with the Daniels and their dog: 'Mrs Daniel acted as cook and kitchen-maid, sometimes assisted by friends, including Rufus, whom I remember polishing the dinner-plates with so much zeal that one day, by a regrettable accident, he licked them all over the stern into deep water. My husband, in the strict privacy of the early morning – mixed bathing not then being tolerated – heroically retrieved them all by repeated dives into the muddy heart of the Thames'.

*Printed in the volume of Bibliography.

HERBERT WARREN

Herbert Warren, Balliol scholar, became President of Magdalen at the age of thirty-two and held that position for forty-three years until 1928. He came into the Daniel Press by old friendship with the printer; several of his poems are about Oxford – 'Addison's Walk', 'May Day on Magdalen Tower' – or translated from the classics and the German, or written for the Daniel family. Poetry must have occupied about fourth place in Warren's energies, but two at least from his Daniel volume, including the title poem, should be printed here:

BY SEVERN SEA

The rolling moorland russet-dun
  With all its gold and purple bloom
Made fragrant by the summer sun,
  Climbs from the softly-curving combe
  Above dark wood and whitening lea
  And orchard green by Severn Sea;

A noble flood, more proudly wide,
  From our deaf island's mother breast
Pours none, nor swirls a fuller tide
  To barter with the boundless West
  For many a costly argosy
  Than this broad stream of Severn Sea.

A dateless gulf whose wave of old
  Yet fervent from the central flame,
By tropic jungle streaming rolled,
  Or foamed around the monstrous frame
  Of flying, creeping, swimming things
  With serpent gorge and dragon wings;

Lands that a mystic glamour fills,
  The after-glow of sunken stars,
Where the old tongues murmur to the hills

Dead loves, dead hates, forgotten wars,
And Arthur's phantom glories haunt
The shadowy scene of high romaunt.

What life, what death of brute and man
Have scarred your earth and stained your wave,
Where pirate horde and robber clan
Have reared and ravaged home and grave,
And gorgeous wrecks of stately Spain
Mix with the bones of Celt and Dane!

Now all is peace from shore to shore,
Mourns Avalon in ruined state
Beneath her silent-watching tor,
And holy Cleeve thy sculptured gate
Sees but the glittering runnel pass
Beside thy cloister-guarded grass;

While towered hall and castle stand,
Their ancient wont and fashion yet
Unchanged, as if some fairy hand
Mid their green oaks of Somerset
Had lulled them to such drowsihood
As chained erewhile the Slumbering Wood,

So sleep they, only through their dream
At times the merry bugles wind,
When hound and horse and horseman gleam
By ferny haunts of hart and hind,
And pride of olden venerie
The antlered stag goes wildly free.

Nought hear they else, but from its well
Deep in the dim heart of the glen
The secret stream from dell to dell
Rustling by ways apart from men,
Till in some cool and shadowed cave
It wed the quiet-waiting wave.

Oh charmèd realm, oh storied scene,
What echoes whisper on your tide,
What memories mingle with your sheen,
Of lives that here have breathed and died,
Of lips whose unforgotten lays
Made beauty lovelier by their praise!

Here sojourned erst the lyric three,
  Whose wandering made a classic ground
From Quantoxhead to Dunkery,
  Where they by height or hollow found
  Fountains that carol for all time
  In tune to their own deathless rhyme;

And here that nearer dearer tongue
  Mourned his dead friend and sang the dirge –
More sadly sweet was never sung –
  Of him who on your murmurous verge
  Wind-wafted from Italian land
  Hath rest by his own Severn strand.

Ah western winds and waters mild!
  Others your vaporous langours chide;
They have not loved you from a child,
  Nor grown to strength your shore beside.
  Ye speak of youth and hope to me,
  Ye airs, ye floods of Severn Sea!

For I was native to your mood
  And apt to take your influence,
To muse and pause, to pore and brood,
  To doubt the shows and shapes of sense,
  To dream how not to dream away
  The long large hours of boyhood's day.

And when high noon on many a sail
  Was bright along the brimming flow,
Or when the westering sun must fail
  Blood-red, and from the shifting glow
  Of lilac-citron skies the queen
  That sways your motion glimmered green,

One lesson still my spirit learned
  From flood and daylight fleeting past,
And from its own strange self that yearned
  Like them to lapse into the vast,
  And merge and end its vague unrest
  In some wide ocean of the West;

Ere we can find true peace again,
  Our being must have second birth,
Purged and made one through toil and pain

With Him Who rules and rounds the earth,
Beyond the dark, behind the light,
In mystery of the Infinite.

And we like rivers from their source
Through cloud and shine, by deep or shoal,
Must follow that which draws our course,
The Love that is its guide and goal;
Of life, of death ye made me free,
Waters and hills of Severn Sea!

THE EVERLASTING NO

Thou who hast seen for once and all the vision,
Thou who hast felt high discontent,
And known the bitter sweet of great ambition
Not for these short-lived follies thou wast meant.

Yet which to follow of the striving voices,
Faith, knowledge, nature, still to meet
Surfeit in pleasure, in faith superstition,
In knowledge weariness, in love deceit?

Forth to the wilderness? Ah I see only
Desert winds shaking the desert reeds:
Ignorant and thirsting still and lonely
Shall solitude suffice my thousand needs?

What though the inner eye be filled with seeing,
What though the mountain and the plain be great,
Only to think and brood in dreams of being,
This cannot solve the riddle of our fate.

Sight of the stars and conscious sense of duty,
These are but drops in the still vacant heart,
These have I known and felt and loved their beauty
With half my soul, nor filled the other part.

A good friend to Daniel's printing, he is a surprising absence from *The Garland of Rachel.* Two slight poems in *By Severn Sea* were written to accompany gifts of the *Shorter Poems* of Robert Bridges. For five years, 1911-16, Warren was Professor of Poetry at Oxford.

LAURENCE BINYON

Binyon was still an undergraduate at Trinity College when he dined with the President and Mrs Woods at their cottage on Boar's Hill in the summer of 1890 to meet Bridges. Five years later his *Poems* were printed at the Daniel Press. 'I have written to Binyon tonight to tell him to send you his poems', Bridges wrote to Daniel in January 1895.* Thus he too joined the small circle of poets, a young man who would have wished now to be remembered as a poet.† Before this early book of poems appeared his British Museum career had begun, in the department of printed books but transferring after two years to the department of prints and drawings.

The importance of that evening with Bridges was mentioned by Nowell Smith,** who wrote that Binyon was fascinated by 'versification: In this he began experimenting while still at Oxford, after meeting Robert Bridges who introduced him to the as yet unpublished poetry of Gerard Manley Hopkins. He followed Bridges and Hopkins in giving the natural stress-accent of English speech a far greater dominance than had been the rule since Chaucer.'

Binyon would provide many slim volumes over the years, and much stout scholarship, but one characteristic in his Daniel poems was near-imitation of Bridges. A London poem, 'The Storm', less successful than 'London Snow' is open imitation. And he offered a self-absorbed ecstasy in the presence of nature, less easy to accept now than then. There remains for us some Keatsian shadow of absurdity in the pre-war England of excessive sensibility – for instance, the end of a poem which begins well, 'May Evening':

*Worcester College correspondence.

†His daughter Nicolete Gray, and son-in-law Basil Gray, have said so with emphasis during questions at a meeting of the Double Crown Club.

***Dictionary of National Biography*.

Till, like the chestnut's languid fans,
I faint beneath that sweet excess.
Delights, that have the edge of pains,
Too fast upon my spirit press.
Darkness, come, and annul desire!
Let me escape into the gloom.
Hide me from sunset's troubling fire,
From this intoxicating bloom!

or the opening of another poem, 'The Elm':

O that I had a tongue that could express
Half of that peace thou ownest, darkling tree!

The Elm is not an absurd poem; we may take pleasure in imagining Keats-Wordsworth aspirations of a young graduate in the eighteen-nineties, unconscious of change unthreatened by war. Such spirits died at Ypres, immortalised in the one poem by Binyon which everyone knows.

Four poems from the Daniel book seem to insist upon their place here: 'Peacefully fresh, O February morn', as an example of his ecstasy, with its prophetic lines:

Now life, with all its hindering riddles, seems
Simple as its own budding to the tree.
Awhile the Fates forbear, and to my dreams,
Sheltered awhile from truth, relinquish me.

'The Storm', as fine in itself and experimenting in the mood of Bridges though missing the miracle of 'London Snow'; 'Fog', in similar vein; and one short perfect poem direct from a moment's observation, 'The Little Dancers'.

Peacefully fresh, O February morn,
The winds come to me: quiet the light slants
Through silver-bosomed clouds, that slowly borne
Across the wide heath, endlessly advance.

Now 'tis that pause before the leaping Spring,
When upon all things waiting comes a hush;
And shyly, listen! the one vocal thing,
Over his dewy notes lingers the thrush.

Now life, with all her hindering riddles, seems
Simple as its own budding to the tree.
Awhile the Fates forbear, and to my dreams,
Sheltered awhile from truth, relinquish me.

In haven and at anchor rides my heart,
And broods upon its swelling joy, apart.

THE STORM

Stooping over London, skies convulsed
With thunder moved: a rumour of storm remote
Hushed them, and birds flew troubled. The gradual clouds
Up from the West climbing, above the East
Glowed sullen as copper embossed: against their gloom,
Like ghosts astonished, thronged the steeples white.
Still with absorbed hurry the streets' uproar
Ran, shadowed by strange unquiet, as vaguely pursued.
Lone workers from drear windows looked and sighed.
Nearer drooped the sky's contracted face;
The face of a Titan in punishment heavily bowed.
As painful sweat, the drops fell loud: at last,
With silent shivering flashes of angry flame,
Long-stifled, his deep thunder burst and groaned.
Till crawling over, the banks of darkness broke
And loosened splendour showered its arrows abroad.
Now, opposite the retreating storm aghast,
In full-recovered sun, new dazzling clouds,
Alp beyond Alp, glitter in awful snow.
Men stop in the street to wonder. The brilliance runs,
Washing with silent waves the town opprest;
Startles squalid rooms with a sudden smile;
Enters gloomy courts, and glories there.
Strange as a vision the wide expanded heavens
Open; the living wind with nearness breathes
On weary faces of women of many cares:
They stand at their doors, and watch with a soothed spirit
The marvellous West asleep in endless light.

FOG

Magically awakened to a strange, brown night
The streets lie cold. A hush of heavy gloom
Dulls the noise of the wheels to a murmur dead:
Near and sudden the passing figures loom;
And out of darkness steep on startled sight
The topless walls in apparition emerge.
Nothing revealing but their own thin flames,
The rayless lamps burn faint and bleared and red:
Link-boys' cries, and the shuffle of horses led,
Pierce the thick air; and like a distant dirge,
Melancholy horns wail from the shrouded Thames.
Long the blind morning hooded the dumb town;
Till lo! in an instant winds arose, and the air
Lifted: at once, from a cold and spectral sky
Appears the sun, and laughs in mockery down
On groping travellers, far from where they deem,
In unconjectured roads; the dwindled stream
Of traffic in slow confusion crawling by;
The baffled hive of helpless man laid bare.

THE LITTLE DANCERS

Lonely, save for a few faint stars, the sky
Dreams; and lonely, below, the little street
Into its gloom retires, secluded and shy.
Scarcely the dumb roar enters this soft retreat;
And all is dark, save where come flooding the rays
From a tavern window: there, to the brisk measure
Of an organ that down in an alley merrily plays,
Two children, all alone and no one by,
Holding their tattered frocks, through an airy maze
Of motion lightly threaded with nimble feet,
Dance sedately: face to face they gaze,
Their eyes shining, grave with a perfect pleasure.

F. W. BOURDILLON

For Bourdillon the Daniel connection was Worcester College; nothing else is traceable now. Eight years younger than Daniel, he went up to Worcester as a scholar. He contributed a poem to *The Garland of Rachel*.

Small volumes of his verse appeared across the rest of his years, including one little-known book (none could be called well-known) in an edition of fifty copies, not mentioned in bibliographies, from the Essex House Press. From 1876 for three years Bourdillon lived at Cumberland Lodge as tutor to two members of the royal family, and for many years at Eastbourne he crammed private pupils for the universities.

One short poem by Bourdillon, 'The night has a thousand eyes', appears in many anthologies; by those eight lines he is remembered. As most poets are not remembered by a single line, that was an achievement. He followed it by many two-stanza poems, which strove without success towards such happy ingenuity of words. Ineffable commonplace flooded each thought which struck him, and this he knew to be so:

> But now my verse, so pondered
> With labour sad and long,
> Strives vainly to be strong.

One is puzzled to think why Daniel printed him, taking on board two books from Bourdillon.* Doubts existed at the time. 'I am sorry if Bourdillon's poems are not good', Bridges wrote to Daniel in October 1889.†

Turning to discover how it once seemed, Bourdillon had a habit of parallels between the visible day and his soul. 'June in London' may stand as a good instance:

**Ailes D'Alouette*, 1890, and (Second Series) 1902.
†Worcester College correspondence.

Sounds of the riverside are in my ear
Through the long day;
The merry haymakers I plainly hear,
The tossing hay.

O cruel dreams that through the roaring town
Mine ears engage!
Alas, poor lark! whose home was once the down,
But now a cage!

Bourdillon as a caged lark does not worry us poetically, but too often his analogies fail, the minor perception is inept. This among his many love poems he called 'Twixt Thee And Me'.

I will not reason why I love,
Or what I love in thee,
There breathes some secret from above
In every flower we see.

Suddenly as we pass we own
Some glimpse or scent divine.
Some secret to none others known
My heart has found in thine.

It will not serve, though better in its scope than most, because no comparison exists between a flower's scent (smellable by anyone who passes) and the private affinity between lovers ('secret to none others known').

There is no purpose at this distance in using a cricket bat against harmless Bourdillon, member of the Athenaeum and of the Alpine Club. 'The Night has a Thousand eyes' appears here of course; with it, from the second flutter of 'Swallow's Wings', four short poems which convey their sense in delicate vein.

THE NIGHT HAS A THOUSAND EYES

The night has a thousand eyes,
And the day but one;
Yet the light of the bright world dies
With the dying sun.

The mind has a thousand eyes,
  And the heart but one;
Yet the light of a whole life dies
  When love is done.

THE WAVE

Roll into gloom!
  Break into white!
Thunder and boom
  In the caverns of night!

Strong is thy wrath,
  Stronger thy fate,
And a wind-blown froth
  Is the end of hate.

A CLAY IMAGE

Till ye can tell me why
Yon cloud-web in the sky
Mocks the lace-weaver's dainty-fingered pain;
Why no inlayer's art
So whispers to the heart
As 'neath the maple the leaf-chequered lane;

I cry against your creed
That Man is Lord indeed,
Judge of his own due and his Maker's duty,
Nor own that ye have wrought
The Godhead of your thought
More true to Deity than Art to Beauty.

A WASTED WORD

I was a fiddler playing
  Alone to a crowded hall;
And what my fingers were saying
  No one knew of them all.

I love you! I love you! I love you! –
  I played it soft and loud;
And you were there and heard it,
  And knew no more than the crowd.

APRIL

In blue and silver came the morning,
  Earth in the lap of Heaven lay,
And I could almost hear the angels
  Who broke the shadows and brought the day.

Every year is the gate of Eden
  Opened, and all the earth made fair;
And every year is the old tale acted,
  And sons of Adam bring sorrow there.

HENRY PATMORE

In 1882 at the age of twenty-two Henry Patmore died of consumption, as had his mother when he was only two years old. The Daniel Press book was done at the suggestion of Edmund Gosse, who wrote to the printer in January 1884: 'My friend Mr Coventry Patmore is proposing to print for private circulation the posthumous poems of his son Henry . . . The poems are really charming'.

Printed affectionately, with a touching introduction by his sister Gertrude and short note by his father, this volume rests within the circle of Daniel poets. A young poet's death from that illness, common in those years, is unknown now. 'Early on the afternoon of February 24th', Gertrude wrote, 'his father sat at his bed-side for the last time, and Henry listened with interest to a proposal that some of his poems should be printed. "I should like it very much", he said'. And Coventry Patmore recalls that once, 'when I had been commending his verses, he laughed and said that I should perhaps be known to future times as "the Father of Patmore"'.

From these slight leavings of a very young man here are three, of which the last was admired by Hopkins, who must have observed especially the final six lines. They closed that book, and this, and after a century may stand as epitaph for all those quiet poets of the Daniel Press.

The thing that makes me patriot most,
Too country-proud to care to boast,
Is not the imperial thought whose pain
Still honours things by Gladstone slain;
And, though the English women are
The pride of peace which wins in war,
And that one who is all my pride
In England seems personified:
The land itself from which she sprung,
These very fields I walk among,
These hills whose sides and gentle tops
Are lit with woods and hung with hops,

Those yellow tracts, and near them seen
So many tints from brown to green, –
This is my country, this the love
No wish can haunt, no pain reprove.

ON A TREE IN A 'WILDERNESS'

From where I sit I often see
A certain tall, misshapen tree;
And, when the wind moans from the West,
It rocks much more than do the rest;
It tosses its unhappy head
Now this way, now that way instead,
Now tries to catch a passing cloud,
Now almost breaks with being bowed;
And all the others bow and nod,
And seem to think it wild and odd.
That ugly indecorous tree
I like, because it seems like me.

PROLOGUE TO POEMS MOSTLY UNWRITTEN

Th' immortal mood was with me then,
That comes but once to mortal men,
The visiting God, whose thronèd place
Is still some maid's unconscious face,
Or blushing, while she wonders why
A man should make a maiden shy.
And him, too much in love to dare
To think he loves her, standing there,
Sharp pain drives thence and angel awe;
And then he sees what there he saw.
For many a man, should this be read,
Will call it his, when I am dead,
And all my words would seem to come
As echoes from his memory dumb.
The care of crooked-counselled time
Returns to love, as verse to rhyme;

And circumstance, which lovers fear,
Is but the dress love deigns to wear,
Which changes variously, and still
Conforms to love, which forms the will.

*Designed and first printed by Sebastian Carter
at the Rampant Lions Press, Cambridge;
set by Monoset Ltd in Monotype Bell;
this edition printed by Call Printers, Cambridge.*